MW01258744

Robert Todd Lincoln's Hildene
and
How It Was Saved
1975 - 1978

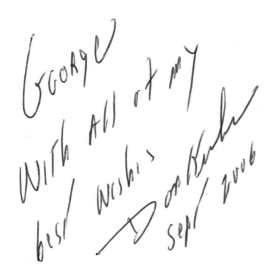

George

With All of my

best wishes

Don Keelan

Sept 2006

Donald B. Keelan

Also by Donald B. Keelan

The Secret of Camp David, Dorrance Publishing, 1995

ISBN: 0-9714931-0-3

Printed at Daamen Inc., Printing Company

Robert Todd Lincoln's Hildene
and
How It Was Saved
1975 - 1978

Donald B. Keelan

DEDICATED
to

My Dear Friend
Oscar

ACKNOWLEDGMENT

The idea to write this book came in the late 1980's. It was during that time that I heard many versions of how Hildene had been saved. Before too many years were to go by, I wanted to collect in one place the recollections, papers and other documents that, when taken together, would form the basis of this story. Furthermore, this story could not have been told without the help and support of many.

Special thanks must go to Judge Arthur O'Dea, for providing me with his time, files and support. And, for opening the doors to other law firms especially that of Edgar Campbell, Esq., who allowed me to do research in his father's files.

The countless hours of interviews with Bob Schmid, Oscar Johnson, the late Ken Hill, James Hickey and Bob Thum became a treasure trove of first-person accounts for which I am deeply grateful.

To those who read the endless drafts and whose suggestions were most helpful and appreciated, goes my thanks. Especially to the late DeWitt "Pete" Copp, Dr. Edward Shaughnessey, Dr. James L. FitzGerald, Colonel Albert C. Jerman, USAF (Ret.) and Nathaniel A. Boone, Esq.

Also, special thanks to Christine Meyer and Anna Bovienzo for typing the countless drafts.

And, finally, thanks and appreciation to the Friends of Hildene for allowing me to do what so many others have done, share the experience of this special place of Vermont and American History.

Donald B. Keelan
Arlington, Vermont
October, 2001

CONTENTS

PREFACE

"The First Church of Christ, Scientist has given local residents of Manchester, Vermont ninety days to come up with a plan to purchase Hildene before offering it to other buyers."

The Wall Street Journal, page 1

July 29, 1976

FORWARD

It is difficult to find the words that in any way could capture the struggle by those few people who saved Hildene.

President Theodore Roosevelt once said,

"Far better it is to dare mighty things, to win glorious triumphs, even though checkered by failure, than to take rank with those poor spirits who neither enjoy nor suffer much, because they live in the gray twilight that knows not victory nor defeat."

INTRODUCTION

In July of 1976 an edict, masked as a challenge, was given to a small group of Manchester, Vermont residents by Mr. Carl Rechner, a real estate consultant for The First Church of Christ Scientist, more commonly known as the Christian Science Church. The peril, so clearly articulated by Rechner at the meeting in the Manchester Town Hall, would soon become the Friends of Hildene's call to action.

It was almost one year since the Church had been informed that Hildene was to go to them, pursuant to Mary (Peggy) Lincoln Beckwith's Will. The Church was meeting for the first time with the Manchester residents. The meeting with representatives from the Church had been anxiously awaited by many in Manchester.

Ever since Peggy's death twelve months prior, rumors were abounding as to what was going to happen to Robert Todd Lincoln's 412-acre estate. The estate included twenty-seven buildings, a 24-room Georgian revival manor house, numerous pieces of furniture, furnishings, equipment and Lincoln family memorabilia.

Not the least of these worries, and probably the most ominous to those who wanted to see the estate preserved, was that the Church was going to dispose of the property. Although there were some local residents who felt this would have been a tragedy, there were others who felt that development would be just fine. There were still others who did not particularly care one way or the other.

Combining the challenge from the Church with the mixed feelings of their neighbors and the lack of money in their accounts, a small band of citizens united under the banner, "Friends of Hildene". What transpired over the next two years is the basis of this story.

Many people who had been involved with Hildene between the period of 1975-1978 wanted to share their recollections. Further, what had proven even more valuable was the opening up of legal files that had been locked away by the seven law firms that had worked on the Mary Lincoln Beckwith Estate. Almost everyone who had a role to play between 1975 and 1978, whether large or small, was asked to recall their experiences.

This story is an attempt to document with as much accuracy and objectivity as is possible, the plight of the original members of the Friends of Hildene to save the historic site from development.

The story touches on the history of the Lincolns and the amazing success that occurred once the Friends of Hildene took over the property.

Hildene is truly a property worth preserving. Its history is told and retold to thousands of visitors each year.

PART I — THE BEGINNING 1975-1976

The United States economy was in the throes of a recession at the time of Peggy Lincoln Beckwith's death in July of 1975. New York City was pleading for financial help from Washington. Its pleas were to fall on deaf ears. Only a half mile from Hildene, the skeleton of the famed Equinox Hotel was a monument to the country's economic woes. The eighteenth century hotel, with its 142 rooms, had been closed and boarded up in 1972 by its creditors. Not unlike other towns in Vermont, Manchester was economically depressed. Its two main sources of income, tourism and manufacturing, were not doing well at all.

Thirty miles north of Manchester, at the Central Vermont Medical Center in Rutland, the last member of the Lincoln family to live at Hildene was waging her final battle. Her courage, wit, intellect and strength were losing out to cancer. At the age of seventy-six, at 2:15 A.M. on July 10, 1975, Mary (Peggy) Lincoln Beckwith died. Before the month was over, her ashes would be returned to her beloved Hildene and, with the help of a close group of friends, spread over the lookout near the formal gardens.

"Peg", as she was known by local Manchester residents, had become the sole mistress of Hildene in 1938 after the death of her Aunt Mary. Her Aunt was the daughter of Robert Todd and Mary Harlan Lincoln. When Robert Todd died in 1926, sole title to Hildene, his summer home that he had built in 1905, was vested in his wife, Mary Harlan. She would continue to live at Hildene during the summers and until her death in 1937. Mary Lincoln Isham, Robert Todd Lincoln's oldest daughter and Peggy's aunt, was given a life estate

1

upon Mary Harlan's death. Mary Lincoln Isham had lived at the nearby 1811 House in Manchester Village. Her tenure at Hildene would not be for long. While in the midst of redecorating the house in 1938, Mary Lincoln Isham died.

One would have thought that the estate should have gone to Peggy's mother, Jessie. However, Robert Todd Lincoln had been outraged over Jessie's marriage to Warren Bechwith and did not look favorably at her eventually owning Hildene. Nevertheless, Jessie, until her death in 1948, did live at Hildene during the summers with her daughter, Peggy. Jessie's winters were often spent with Robert Lincoln Beckwith, Peggy's younger brother, at his plantation in Woodstock, Virginia. Mary and Jessie's brother, Abraham Lincoln II, was never part of the Will because he had died from blood poisoning in 1890.

Peggy had always loved Hildene and thoroughly enjoyed her thirty-seven year reign as its mistress. The concrete slabs of airplane hangers, the last remnants of her days of flying her bi-plane from the Hildene meadows in the late 1920's and 1930's, can still be seen today. Hildene and its magnificent topography with flowers and specimen trees became the subject of her photography and painting skills. Earlier, Peggy had taken up golf where her grandfather left off - - just outside the front door to the main house as well as down the road at the Ekwanok Country Club. Her grandfather, Robert Todd Lincoln, had been President of the Club for twenty years and on April 4, 1918, he transferred two shares of the Club's stock to her. The Ekwanok, in 1977, would redeem the two shares for $10.

Unlike her grandfather, Peggy had befriended many of the local people. She made it her business to get out and visit and in time, she

2

formed a close circle of friends. She never married. These friends became her 'family'.

Before taking over Hildene, Peggy acquired her own hideaway in the mid-1930s. It was located in the foothills of the mountains north of the Manchester Country Club. It was a sixty-acre estate with a large pond. Peggy had built a comfortable building made from the wood siding of an old barn on the site. She called her hideaway "Bull's Head." Some years later, Peggy formed an association with her friends called The Bull's Head Foundation. Some of the members in The Bull's Head Foundation would later, in 1976, form the nucleus of what would ultimately become the Friends of Hildene.

One question is frequently asked. If there was already in existence a group of friends and a Foundation, why then did Hildene and most of the balance of Peggy's estate go to the Church and not to the Friends of Hildene?

The answer is on the one hand quite basic and on the other complex. To see why, we must go back in time to Peggy's grandmother, Mary Harlan Lincoln.

· ·

Robert Todd Lincoln, the only one of Abraham and Mary Todd Lincoln's four sons who lived to maturity, married Mary Harlan on September 24, 1868 in Washington, District of Columbia. The daughter of James Harlan, a respected United States Senator from Mt. Pleasant, Iowa, Mary was intelligent, independent and wealthy in her own right.

Having recognized early on that she would be living in the shadows of her famous husband and revered late father-in-law, Abraham Lincoln, Mary Harlan Lincoln developed her own interests and friends. One of her earliest and closest friends was Mary Morse Baker Eddy, the founder and spiritual leader of the Christian Science Church. Thus began a relationship that went on for thirty years until Mary Eddy's death in 1910.

Mary Harlan Lincoln deeply believed in the tenets of the Church. She felt that Eddy was correct in her preaching that the mind and not the body was what needed to be treated when illness occurred. Her husband, Robert, did not share her belief. For that matter, Peggy shared Mary's beliefs only minimally. Nevertheless, Mary Harlan stated in her Will that upon the death of the last of her descendants, one-third of the assets that remained of the estate were to be passed on to the Church. The other two-thirds were to be divided between the American Red Cross and Iowa Wesleyan College of Mt. Pleasant, Iowa. The assets involved were quite substantial.

Peggy's grandfather, Robert Todd Lincoln, had come into a modest inheritance when his father, Abraham Lincoln, was killed. At the time, Robert was still a Captain in the Union Army. The death of his father on April 14, 1865 made him a one-third heir of Abraham Lincoln's $110,000 estate. He would share this estate with his mother and younger brother Thomas (Tad). Tragedy would strike the Lincoln family once again. In 1871, while Robert Todd was engaged in the practice of law, word came that his brother Tad had succumbed to pleurisy at the age of eighteen.

Robert's wealth grew because of his skillful practice of law, his association with the industry titans of the day and his close professional and personal relationship with George Mortimer Pullman. His relationship with Pullman, the inventor and founder of the Pullman Palace Car Company, began in 1872. In 1892, Robert Todd was appointed special counsel to the Pullman Company. At the time of his death, in 1897, George Pullman's company was the largest manufacturer of railroad cars in the country.

The leadership void at the Pullman Company created by its founder's death was filled when Robert Todd was elected Pullman's President in 1901. Later, in 1911, he became Chairman of the Board of Directors. He served on the Board until his death in 1926.

In 1902, during his tenure at the Pullman Company and his partnership years with the law firm of Isham, Lincoln and Beale of Chicago (actually, ever since the death of his son, Abraham Lincoln II, ten years earlier), Robert Todd did not practice law. He put together many parcels of land in Manchester, Vermont to form the site for his family's summer residence. He had been to Manchester's Equinox Hotel with his mother and her close friend and traveling companion, Mrs. Abner Doubleday, in May of 1863 and again in 1864. It had been his visits to his law partner Isham's summer home, now known as Ormsby Hill, in Manchester that renewed his interest in Vermont.

. . . .

The building of his 24-room Georgian revival mansion for $63,000 together with numerous ancillary buildings, enabled Robert Todd and his wife, Mary, to escape the attention they had encountered in their Washington, DC and Chicago homes. It became a ritual each May, from 1905 until his death, for Robert Todd Lincoln to come to Manchester Depot in his private railroad car, often followed by a dozen or more servants, to open up Hildene. They would leave before the first snow.

The size of the main house and the lush gardens that surrounded it, together with their staff, would suggest that the Lincolns

5

anticipated constantly entertaining their friends. Quite the contrary! It was at Hildene that Robert Todd enjoyed and protected his privacy ferociously. Receiving visitors was held to a minimum during the twenty-one years he spent there.

．．．．．．．．．．．．．．．．．．．．．

Robert Todd died at Hildene on July 25, 1926. At the time of his death he was being attended to by his close friend and physician, Dr. Claude Campbell. Neither man knew the important role that Dr. Campbell's son, Jim, a lawyer, would have decades later at Hildene with Robert Todd's granddaughter, Peggy.

Few people have any idea of the disparity of wealth that existed between Abraham Lincoln and his son Robert.

Robert Todd Lincoln's estate in 1926 was valued at approximately $3 million. An amount that, in the year 2001 would equate to over thirty million dollars. A substantial portion of his estate was left to his wife, Mary Harlan Lincoln.

．．．．．．．．．．．．．．．．．．．．．

On December 30, 1935 at the office of her Washington, D.C. attorney, Mary Harlan Lincoln executed her Last Will and Testament. One of the three witnesses to the signing was a youthful attorney named Elizabeth R. Young, who would play an important role in the transferring of her client's property to the Friends of Hildene forty years later.

Mary Harlan Lincoln's Will was explicit regarding her intentions for the disposition of her husband's Hildene.

It contained the following paragraph:

*'My real estate known as "Hildene", at Manchester,
Vermont, together with all improvements thereon, all farm and
other implements, and all furnishings, bric-a-brac, books, pic-
tures and silverware (excepting the President Lincoln silverware
which, by paragraph "FIRST" hereof I have bequeathed unto my
daughter, MARY LINCOLN ISHAM), contained in the buildings, I give, devise and bequeath unto my granddaughter, MARY
LINCOLN BECKWITH, in full and perfect ownership.'*

The Will continued to carry forward the wishes of Robert Todd
Lincoln to disinherit their daughter Jessie, Mary did however make
one or two exceptions to her husband's wishes. She wanted Jessie to
own all of her automobiles as well as half of a Trust Fund. In the event
that none of her three grandchildren produced any children and did
not survive Mary Lincoln Isham or Jessie Lincoln Beckwith Randolph
(the name of Randolph was Jessie's third husband), all of her estate
with the exception of Hildene, was to go to her daughter, Jessie.

The issue of what to do with Hildene had been addressed by
Mary Harlan Lincoln fifteen months earlier in a letter to her daughter
Jessie. On September 29, 1934, she wrote a seven page handwritten
letter to 'Petticoat', her nickname for Jessie. In the letter she attempt-
ed to eliminate any feelings that Jessie might have had regarding
things she might have said or done in the past that would have
angered her mother and father so much that she was being disinherit-
ed. Mary Harlan told Jessie that she and Papa (Robert Todd Lincoln)
had discussed giving Hildene to 'Peg' many years ago. Robert Todd
Lincoln was concerned about her being "steady enough" because of her
age. Peggy must have been in her mid-twenties when Robert Todd
Lincoln made that remark. Mary Harlan said to her daughter that
much thought went into her decision to give the property to her oldest
daughter (Mary) and then to Peggy. She went on to write:

... I decided our eldest child
should properly inherit the
place, certainly for her
lifetime, and I gave
instructions that this be
done, but that the
property on Mamie's death,
should go to Peg, for good
and all — I did not as
you suggest in your last
letter, surround the property
with a "trust" — It will
be Peggy's, absolutely —

Nothing you have done,
ever, has had any in-
fluence with me in the
making of my Will, and
I think Hildene is dealt
with, as Papa could have liked —

I have simply
tried to be as fair as I
could be to all of my
family, without fear, or favor —
as my present will
is now four years old,

I think it is evident
that nothing you have
said, or done, has had
anything to do with the
manner in which I
dealt with Hildene, at
that time — ....

The Will was modified within six months. A Codicil was added on June 15, 1936, eleven months prior to Mary Harlan Lincoln's death. The ninety-year old widow of Robert Todd Lincoln changed her intentions regarding Hildene. Her Codicil gave a life estate in Hildene to her daughter, Mary Lincoln Isham, and upon her death the property would go directly to her granddaughter Peggy. This action was noted in a decree of the Manchester, Vermont Probate Court on July 7, 1938 and recorded for posterity in Volume 39, page 375 of the Manchester Land Records. Within two years complete ownership of Hildene would pass to Peggy and remain there until it was transferred by death to the Church, almost forty years later.

· ·

In 1975, Manchester, Vermont had a population of approximately 2,500 and was not known as a center for the practice of law. There were few law firms in town, maybe five or six.

One such firm was James B. Campbell, Esq. Campbell, a native of Manchester, was educated in the local schools and was a graduate of Dartmouth College and George Washington University Law School. Campbell's family was well known to the Lincolns of Manchester. Jim Campbell's father, Claude Campbell, was Robert Todd Lincoln's physician and a trusted friend.

It was little wonder that Peggy would engage the son of her grandfather's doctor to handle her legal affairs. Campbell's office in the center of Manchester was in many ways in stark contrast to the law firms that Peggy's ancestors engaged. Peggy had spent almost all of her life in Manchester. She knew many of its residents and, more importantly, she felt at ease with them. However, Peggy was not totally free to deal solely with local attorneys and bankers. Part of the estate she had inherited in 1938 was in stocks and bonds, investment instruments in which she had very little patience for understanding. Accordingly, she allowed the management of them to be done by City Bank Farmer's Trust Company (now known as Citi-Corp) on Park Avenue in New York City as well as by American Security and Trust Company located a block away from the White House in Washington, D.C., where Trusts her grandmother had established were being managed.

On September 5, 1950, Peggy executed her Last Will and Testament. In doing so, she appointed City Bank Farmer's Trust Company and her attorney, James B. Campbell, to be co-executors and the trustees of her estate. They would work for a fee of 3% of gross estate and a 3% commission of the annual gross income.

Twenty-five years later, on July 11, 1975, the day after Peggy's death, Jim Campbell wrote to Mr. Sydney Schneck, a Vice President at First National City Bank (the C.B.F's.T Co. had been renamed), to inform the Bank of their role pursuant to Peggy's Will. Campbell's letter also described that Peggy's house in Manchester was "in a poor state of repair" and there would be a requirement to maintain the existing staff of seven employees. He went on to tell Mr. Schneck that he had no idea of the size of the estate in that certain trust funds were held by the bank as well as by American Security. However, the most significant portion of Campbell's letter concerned the fact that Peggy had him draft a new Will in 1974. She never signed it.

The fact that Peggy had been in the process of revising her Will, was also known by at least two of her close friends in Manchester. They were, Oscar V. Johnson, Jr., her immediate neighbor who was both a farmer and owner of a local fuel oil business, and Ken Hill, a trusted employee whom she had hired in 1947. Both men, together with several of Peggy's other close friends, would later play a key role in the forming of the Friends of Hildene. It was their intimate knowledge of Peggy's intentions that drove them so hard after her death to acquire Hildene as a memorial to her mother and grandparents.

Attorney Campbell was indeed in possession of a draft Will. However, from a legal standpoint, he had to abide by Peggy's September 5, 1950 Last Will and Testament.

In addition to the draft of a Will he made for Peggy, Campbell was also aware of an earlier memorandum he had given her regarding the disposition of Hildene.

That memorandum included the details of a proposed transfer of Hildene's real estate from Peggy to the State of Vermont. It was based on Chapter 186 of the Vermont Statutes (revised in 1947) Section 4171. The proposal was for the State of Vermont to take over the property and operate it both as a farm and a museum.

The memorandum stated Peggy's reasons for considering the State of Vermont as the recipient of Hildene:

The dwelling house and much of its contents have his-

toric significance through association with the Lincoln family. The land is suitae for various types of farming, and has numerous varieties of trees and shrubs growing on it.

Donor desires to have the property preserved, insofar as possible, and objects to its commercial development by private parties after her death. She is interested in its development and management after her death in a manner consistent with the welfare of the Town of Manchester and the people of the State of Vermont.

Over the years the property has become a 'game refuge', and on certain portions wild life, songbirds and game birds are plentiful. The gardens contain many varieties of bulbs, plants and flowers.

She never followed through on the memorandum. She would have many other plans for Hildene, but by July 1975 it was too late.

. . . .

After Peggy's death Attorney James Campbell, now the co-executor of Peggy's estate, had to deal with hunters. Hildene, with its four hundred twelve acres of cornfields, marshes, forests and frontage on the Battenkill River was and continues to be a rich habitat for wildlife.

In 1975 it was also a hunter's dream to be able to take small game and, for a few weeks in November, deer from within Hildene's boundaries. While only a small fraction of Vermont's land was restricted to hunters, more commonly known as "posted", Hildene was a part of that small fraction. However, the Hill family, David Conners, George Hoag and Howard Brophy, all local residents, did hold hunting permits from Peggy. Jim Campbell noted in a September 17, 1975 letter to his co-executor, Emil Lemay of Citibank, that he canceled the permits so as not to have hunters roaming around the now vacant property.

. . . .

Attorney Campbell's office became inundated with letters from individuals and organizations from around the country requesting an opportunity to visit Hildene and pour through the Lincoln memorabilia. Before Peggy's Will was entered into Probate on August 23, 1975, requests to photograph the interior of the main house came from newspapers as well as television stations. Campbell fended off all of the requests. He did so quite diplomatically in keeping with his own well-known private demeanor.

Requests for visits or for items from the estate came from organizations as well as individuals. One such request came from the Bi-Centennial Commission of the Town of Manchester. Their interest was to acquire from the estate the "River Road Schoolhouse." This one-room historic building was located on the easterly side of River Road. It was officially known as School District Number Ten and locally known as the Hollow School. It was first occupied in 1832 and, for almost sixty-five years, was used to educate local children. The Town of Manchester's request was turned over to the Church by Jim Campbell and was never acted upon. The Friends of Hildene had the schoolhouse completely restored in 1983.

What made the Town's request unusual was the fact that on August 17, 1909, the schoolhouse had been conveyed by Robert Todd Lincoln to Manchester. This conveyance was recorded in Item 10 of the Abstract of Conveyances. At least that is what Campbell told the

13

Commission. In fact, Manchester had conveyed the property to Robert Todd Lincoln in 1909. It was located on the old Walker Farm and he wanted the title to the school house.

Two weeks after Peggy's death, the Governor of Kentucky, Julian M. Carroll, became personally involved. On July 24, 1975 he wrote to Jim Campbell. The purpose was to inform Campbell that he would appreciate it if Campbell would provide assistance to Beula Cornelius Nunn, the wife of Kentucky's former governor who was chairperson of the Mary Todd Lincoln Foundation at that time. The Foundation had recently restored the Mary Todd Lincoln House and the Parker House in Lexington, Kentucky, as well as several other Lincoln homes in Kentucky. Mrs. Nunn was also a trustee in the newly opened Lincoln Memorial University located near the Cumberland Gap in Harrogate, Tennessee.

Jim Campbell took no action. He had enough to do just marshalling the estate's assets soon after the death of his client and friend. Mrs. Nunn was willing to wait, for a while anyway. Early in 1976, she obtained permission to gain access to Hildene. On Sunday, February 29, 1976, accompanied by Dr. Frank Rankin who was the Chairman of the Board of Trustees of Lincoln Memorial University (LMU), Nunn's quest brought her and Rankin to Hildene. Rankin was in receipt of a half million-dollar gift from "Colonel" Harlan Sanders of Kentucky Fried Chicken fame to build a new library at LMU. He wanted as much Lincoln memorabilia as he could obtain. Hildene, he had heard, was a treasure trove.

A year later, on April 1, 1977, Mrs. Nunn would be quoted in Lexington, Kentucky's The Lexington Leader, asking:

If they [the Church] did not operate Hildene as a Shrine could the personal property be moved to a shrine in Kentucky?

Dr. Rankin and Mrs. Nunn went through the house, from cellar to attic. It was in the attic that she found a portrait of Levi Todd, the founder of Lexington. She was ecstatic. She was quoted as saying:

When I walked in that big hall there were goose pimples all over me.

It was quite understandable to sense the feeling of exhilaration that must have come over both Kentuckians. Rankin found a trunk that contained gifts the Lincolns had received while Abraham Lincoln was President. Mrs. Nunn said:

I wanted everything that pertained to Mary Todd Lincoln and the Todd family to be in Lexington.

According to correspondence between Mrs. Nunn and Campbell, as well as between Mrs. Nunn and Glenn S. Kenngott of the Church, her intentions were quite clear and specific. She wanted all of Hildene's furnishings and personal property to be donated by the Christian Science Church to her Kentucky foundation, specifically to the Parker House, to the Todd House, and to the University. Mrs. Nunn wrote in her March 12, 1976 letter to Kenngott that if a donation was not practical, her organization would be willing to pay for the historic items at their appraised value.

Mrs. Nunn went on to say in her letter:

Words cannot express the warmth that would pour from our hearts and that of all people.

The Christian Science Church did not acquiesce to the wishes of Mrs. Nunn. She was persistent, however, and moved on to petition Peggy's brother, Robert Lincoln Beckwith. In doing so, she obtained a small degree of success. It had taken her six months, but through the intervention of some mutual friends, she finally met Robert Todd Lincoln Beckwith.

The mutual friends were Mr. and Mrs. Fred Schwengle. They had dinner with her at a fashionable Washington, D.C. club in February, 1977. According to Mrs. Nunn, Beckwith hardly said a word. It wasn't until someone suggested that Beckwith and Nunn adjourn to the club's library to be by themselves that he did open up. Nunn said Beckwith told her she could have certain items for the Mary Todd Lincoln House.

On February 23, 1977, Robert executed an agreement with the Kentucky Mansions Preservation Foundation, Inc. In the agreement, Robert stipulated that certain things he inherited from his sister had belonged to his great grandmother, Mary Todd Lincoln.

Accordingly, the agreement conveyed the following to the Kentucky group:

Silver Mounted Glass Decanter; Smoking Set;

Two George III Silver Wine Funnels;

Silver Dressing Articles; Group Table Articles;

Silver Plated Cut Glass Inkwell;

Assembled Dresden Gamiture; Pair of Dresden Vases

Not included in Mrs. Nunn's wish list were the following items, which she had strongly believed were from the Todd homes of Lexington:

Grandfather Clock

Drum Desk

Set of Six (6) Candlesticks; Presentation Bowl;

Silver Tea Service

Dresden Onion Dessert Plates

Nineteen (19) Spode Cream Soups

Pair Cast Iron Candlesticks

In 1977, James Hickey was Robert Beckwith's agent and curator of the Lincoln Collection at the Illinois State Historical Library. Hickey said that none of the items that were given to Mrs. Nunn by Beckwith had their origin in Kentucky. All of them were either acquired by Robert Todd Lincoln or by his wife, Mary Harlan.

Most of Hildene's furnishings and the family's personal effects are still at Hildene. If the Church had given in to Mrs. Nunn's original request, the success of the Friends of Hildene, might never have been possible.

This incident, unbeknownst to the Friends of Hildene at the time, was just one in a series of near tragedies that would fall upon them over the next two and a half years in their struggle to save Hildene.

· ·

In addition to securing Hildene from hunters, Jim Campbell had a score of other immediate tasks that faced him as Peggy's co-executor. The most pressing was the welfare of Hildene's employees.

They were: Ken Hill, Erroll Hill, David Connors, Marie Peirson, Charles L. Thompson, Mary Thompson and Dorothy Squires.

In the Summer of 1975, Ken Hill, as caretaker, was in charge of Hildene's staff, several of whom had lived on the estate for many years. Peggy had hired Ken about thirty years previously. Over the ensuing years, he and his wife, Lois, together with their sons, Brian and Erroll, and daughter-in-law, Susan, became Peggy's closest friends. As if he were repaying his dear, departed friend for the many benefits she had bestowed upon him, Ken and his family would play a key role in preserving Hildene over the next two years. The immediate problem facing Ken, however, was how to pay all of the employees and direct them in their caretaker roles until such time as Campbell could transfer ownership of Hildene to the Church.

Campbell wrote to his co-executor, Emil Lemay, on August 4, 1975. He informed Lemay that Robert Lincoln Beckwith was paying the employees. In light of the fact that no pension plan had been established for them, Beckwith verbally indicated to them that he would like to initiate something.

Peggy's 1950 Will had made no provisions for her employees. She never got around to stating her wishes for them in the draft of the Will dated February 20, 1974. Robert Lincoln Beckwith was repaid $5,593.44 on September 12, 1975. This reimbursement covered payments to the six employees from July 17 to August 25, 1975. After the last payroll of August 25th the estate staff was reduced to Ken Hill, caretaker, and his son, Erroll, assistant caretaker. Severance pay equaling three weeks of wages was given to the discharged employees.

· ·

August 23, 1975 was an important date to all parties who had

18

any interest in Peggy's estate. On that date, Campbell presented Peggy's Will for a probate hearing before Probate Judge Margaret Dougherty. Three weeks prior, on August 1, he filed Peggy's Will with the Court. This legal ceremony brought Peggy's estate under the umbrella of Vermont's legal system. Also, probate is an event that provides the public access to the intentions of the deceased.

The probating of Mary Lincoln Beckwith's Will did not garner a great deal of attention. Locally, other events were being discussed. One topic was the Mattusen Associates consulting firm report, which had favored that the Village of Manchester and the Town of Manchester should merge. This was followed by the news out of Washington, D.C. that the U.S. Supreme Court was not going to hear the case on approving the new Route 7 because there had not been an environmental impact statement. Oscar Johnson's appointment as the 4th Chairman of the Mark Skinner Library, had been given more local press coverage than that of Peggy's Will.

Later, on November 10, 1975, appointment powers were given. Judge Doughtery named Ken Hill and Doug Shaw as Commissioners and Appraisers for the estate. In Fall 1975, Ken Hill and Doug Shaw saw Hildene's twenty-seven buildings in every imaginable physical condition along with many pieces of farm equipment and implements. The land ranged from grassy meadows, cornfields and forests to rocky cliffs that dropped off two hundred feet. The marshalling of the estate assets began. Appraisals were underway. Doug Shaw was and continues to this day to be a highly respected real estate appraiser. His task was not an easy one by any means. Hildene was a twenty-four room Georgian revival mansion located on a beautiful promontory overlooking 412 acres. Many had believed that the estate had been larger. The Boston Globe reported on August 24, 1975 that Peggy had left her 1,000 acre estate together with $425,000 to the Christian Science Church. Also, the Lexington Leader on April 1, 1977, described the main house as having 42 rooms.

Shaw was up to the task. On March 26, 1976 he filed his appraisal with the Court:

412 acres land	. . .$371,000.00
Main Dwelling (Hildene)	. . . .100,000.00
Private Art Studio	. . . . . .3,000.00
Carriage House	. . . . .25,000.00
Main Farm House	. . . . .46,000.00
Guest House (storage)	. . . . . .4,000.00
Small Garage	. . . . . . .500.00
Horse Barn	. . . . . .9,700.00
Main Dairy Barn	. . . . .15,000.00
Machine Storage Barn	. . . . . .5,000.00
Open Cattle Shed	. . . . . .2,000.00
Slaughter House Garage	. . . . . . .500.00
Corn Crib Grainery	. . . . . . .500.00
North Farm House	. . . . .42,500.00
Red School House	. . . . . .2,500.00
Total Real Estate	**. $627,200.00**

In addition to the real estate, Shaw assigned a value of $12,785 to the personal property which was made up of cars, tractors and other equipment.

Shaw's report went on to describe each of the buildings that he had appraised. Many had not been included because of their condition, particularly the buildings adjacent to the Carriage Barn.

Shaw's $100,000 appraisal value for the main house was exceptionally low, even in 1975 values. Comments such as "seriously damaged" and "in bad general condition having had no extensive work performed for a great number of years" peppered his report.

Doug Shaw was not qualified to appraise the Hildene furniture, paintings, manuscripts and papers as well as other Lincoln family mementos. Campbell's co-executor, Emil Lemay of CitiBank, had assigned this task to the New York City firm of Masterson-O'Connell Company, Inc.

On October 22, 1975, in a sworn affidavit made out to the Internal Revenue Service, Mr. Charlton M. Theus, Jr. of the O'Connell firm declared that the estate's personal property was valued at $26,820. His fifty-two-page inventory listed $3,565 worth of property, between pages one to nine, as being bequeathed to Robert Todd Lincoln Beckwith and the balance, $23,255, willed to the Christian Science Church.

Was the Masterson-O'Connell appraisal thorough? How realistic were the values they used? It can be debated ad infinitum. Both the value of $150 assigned to the thirty-five trunks located in the attic and the value of $270 assigned to the six rifles, shotguns and pistols appeared to be low. The same argument most likely can be made about the Shaw appraisal. Why were the dollar values set so low in light of the fact that there would be little or no estate taxes? It is a mystery to this day.

Nevertheless, the Shaw appraisal would, later on, become the basis for the Church's soliciting of offers from interested purchasers. Ten months later, the amount represented an almost impossible obstacle for The Friends of Hildene to overcome in their drive to preserve the property.

. . . .

On October 17, 1975 Robert and Mary Colonna Schmid wrote a letter to Jim Campbell. Bob and his wife, Mary, lived opposite Route 7 (today Route 7A) from Hildene. Mary Colonna was Peggy Beckwith's distant cousin as well as close friend and a frequent visitor to Hildene. Her family ties went back to Robert Todd Lincoln's law partner, Edward S. Isham. Edward S. Isham was Mary's great grandfather. Also, Robert Todd Lincoln's daughter (Mary Lincoln Isham) was Schmid's godmother. Mary Colonna's mother, Frances Isham Colonna, was Peggy's childhood playmate. To Frances, Beckwith was known as Cousin Peg or CP.

Little did Bob Schmid know then, that over the next two and a half years he would be involved in the writing of hundreds of pieces of correspondence in connection with his interest in the preservation of Hildene.

Several months after Peggy's death, Bob and Mary wrote to Jim Campbell to express their deep feelings that Hildene be preserved as a memorial to the Lincoln family. The correspondence mentioned that, if necessary, they would obtain the signatures of Manchester towns-people in order for the Schmid's to press their case with the Church through Jim Campbell's office. The Schmid's had hoped that Campbell would use his position as co-executor to convince the Church that they must make a "truly whole hearted effort to keep the lands intact."

The Schmid's letter to Campbell had been motivated by the fact that on October 2, 1975, representatives from the Church were at Hildene and were quoted in the Manchester Journal as having said:

no use has been decided [for the property] until inventoried, surveyed and probated.

Jim Campbell had a great deal of respect for Bob Schmid, a former Vice President of the Ford Foundation. However, it was Campbell's task to administer the estate with the ultimate goal of having Hildene transferred to the Church. The Schmids must have had a premonition of what was to become of Hildene if it were to be given to the Church. In July of the following year, their worst fears would be realized.

· ·

In the fall of 1975, Jim Campbell's small law offices were deluged with requests from all over the country requesting from the Beckwith estate information, artifacts, visits and examination of historical papers. They also wanted parts of the estate's tangible property.

Even though Campbell was now deeply involved in the administration of the estate, particularly in obtaining all of the information needed to prepare the U.S. Estate Tax form for filing in the Spring, he still took the time to answer each letter.

On August 27, 1975, a request came from as far away as Iowa, the home state of Peggy's grandmother, Mary Harlan Lincoln. Joyce Giaquinta, the manuscript Librarian of the Iowa State Historical Department, wanted to know if there were any James Harlan papers still at Hildene. Harlan was Robert Todd Lincoln's father-in-law and Iowa's U.S. Senator.

A few days earlier, another letter had been received from Thomas Welles Brainard of Woodstock, Connecticut. At the request of Clara May Hemenway, Manchester's Town Clerk and a close friend of Peggy's, Brainard wrote to Campbell to ask if Peggy had in her possession any letters from her grandfather, Robert Todd Lincoln. Thomas

Welles Brainard, was the great, great grandson of an Abraham Lincoln Cabinet appointee, Gideon Welles, and his grandfather had been a close friend to Robert Todd Lincoln when the latter was at the Pullman Company.

Politely, on August 28, 1975, Jim Campbell wrote to inform the Connecticut resident that it would be months before the estate knew what it had. He also informed Brainard that Robert Lincoln Beckwith's address was not available. He conveyed the same message to the folks at the Iowa State Historical Department.

As the estate moved along the probate highway, additional requests for information were being made to Jim Campbell. One was a letter he received on August 28, 1975 from a California attorney named Andrew Collins. It appeared that Peggy's father Warren Beckwith remarried and had a son from that marriage, Warren Beckwith, Jr. That would make Mr. Beckwith of LaJolla, California a half brother to Peggy. Campbell responded to the letter and forwarded a copy of Peggy's Will to Attorney Collins. Nothing more was ever heard from the Beckwith's of California.

· ·

At the time of Peggy's death the only living descendant of Abraham Lincoln was her brother, Robert Lincoln Beckwith. When his sister died, he was living on his estate in Saludo, Virginia. Having realized at an earlier time that one day he would become the heir to some of his grandfather's, as well as great grandfather's papers and personal items, Robert Lincoln Beckwith began to develop a relationship with a James Hickey in 1965.

James Hickey was the curator of the Lincoln Collection for the Illinois State Historical Library in Springfield, Illinois. He had met

Bob Beckwith in 1965 when the Historical Library was hosting a celebration marking the 100th anniversary of the end of the Civil War. Because Hickey was one of the newest people working for the Library, he was given the task of escorting Beckwith.

By maintaining his relationship with Robert Lincoln 'Bud' Beckwith, Hickey was able to achieve two goals. He was able to act as an advisor to the last of the Lincolns in order to protect Beckwith's interests. He was also able to be in a position to preserve for generations to come Abraham Lincoln's papers, works of art as well as other memorabilia.

Beckwith was always interested in visiting his sister at Hildene for personal reasons. Following her death, he traveled to Hildene accompanied by Hickey to inspect, inventory and direct the shipment of those items that were given to him through the Will.

It was always his contention as well as that of James Hickey that there was a distinction between possessions and estate personal property. As an immediate member of the family he was entitled to certain tangible property on the basis that it was personal. Accordingly, such items were not part of the estate inventory. One such item was a set of model trains that was at Hildene from the time he visited his grandfather. A more sensitive area concerned his sister's paintings. Mr. Hickey, in a letter to Jim Campbell dated September 15, 1977, made the strong case for his client that Peggy wanted her brother to have her paintings and that according to RT Bud Beckwith, certain unfinished paintings by his sister were to be destroyed.

Hickey would come back to visit Hildene on several other occasions. On one such occasion, while looking over old papers in what is known as the file room, just off Robert Todd Lincoln's office and bedroom, he concluded that there had to be more documents and papers around.

In a double locked closet in Robert Todd Lincoln's bedroom was Robert Todd Lincoln's set of documents pertaining to the insanity trial of Mrs. Abraham Lincoln. The discovery of these papers at Hildene took on major significance. Firstly, the official papers of the State of Illinois had either been lost, partially destroyed or were not comprehensive. Secondly, Nicholas Murray Butler, the noted historian and academician who was also an acquaintance friend of Robert Todd Lincoln, had noted in his writings that he had witnessed, in 1923, Robert Todd Lincoln destroy Abraham Lincoln's papers in the library fireplace, at Hildene.

Butler's observation was later clearly proven to have been mistaken. In 1947, The Library of Congress in Washington, D.C., opened the eight trunks which Robert Todd Lincoln previously had in his possession; there were originally only six trunks. In 1909 Robert Todd Lincoln had his secretary repack them —the result required two more trunks which he had given to the Library of Congress in a secret arrangement in 1919. For the first time, the world saw Abraham Lincoln's papers. Butler, the former President of Columbia University, recanted his story by stating that it had been the insanity trial papers of Mrs. Abraham Lincoln that he had seen destroyed in 1923 at Hildene by Robert Todd Lincoln. James Hickey, together with Ken Hill and his son Errol, found the insanity trial papers and had them shipped to Beckwith's home and, at a later date, transferred to Springfield. Since then, scholarly research has produced a book dealing with the trial and Robert Todd Lincoln's role in it. (Insanity File: The Case of Mary Todd Lincoln by Mark E. Neely, Jr. and R. Gerald

McMurtry, published by Southern Illinois University Press.)

Notwithstanding this rare discovery, Hickey would continue to play a significant role during the next year and a half as the Friends of Hildene negotiated the acquisition of the property.

North side view of Hildene in July 1975.

South view at time of Peggy's death.

Bob Schmid, Hildene's first Chairman, at Visitors Center, in July 1989.

PART II • CREATION OF THE FRIENDS OF HILDENE

The winter and spring of 1976 found the Church busy determining exactly what it was going to do with Hildene and the 412-acre estate.

If the Church had doubts about what to do with the real estate Peggy Beckwith had left them, there were no such concerns with the balance of the estate, especially the nine hundred thousand dollars in bonds and stocks.

On April 1, 1976, Emil Lemay, an Assistant Vice President of First National City Bank, and James Campbell, both the co-executors of Peggy's estate, filed with the Internal Revenue Service a twenty-three page Estate Tax Return. For Campbell, this filing must have been one of the largest in his legal career. Peggy did not die a poor woman. The Return listed the gross estate as having a value of $1,666,215.51. The sum was broken down as follows:

Hildene, real estate and buildings	$ 627,200
Stocks, bonds, and preferred stocks	908,480
Mortgages, cash and notes	60,089
Furnishings	23,255
Farm equipment	12,785
Other	34,406
TOTAL	$ 1 666,215

• •

The estate had to be reduced by approximately $30,059 from debt. The largest being a $25,000 note to Factory Point National Bank.

The filing listed additional funds that would go to the Church.

29

Peggy, in her 1950 Will, had directed that a trust fund be set up and funded by $425,000. The lifetime beneficiaries of the trust were to have been:

- Robert J. Randolph
- Henry Todd
- Bessie C. Reely
- Phoebe Bushee
- Florence Anthony
- Grace Portious

This group included distant relatives, servants and friends. The amounts they were to have received ranged from $416 to $20 per month. Grace Portious, who lived in England, was to get $38 worth of food shipped to her home each month. By July 10, 1975, the date of Peggy's death, they all were dead. The co-executors with the help of Attorney Elizabeth Young in Washington, D.C., spent a considerable amount of time tracking them down. The $425,000 trust fund would not be needed. Instead, it would go to the Church in addition to their original bequest of $425,000.

The estate filing listed three other heirs in addition to the Church and they were to receive the following:

Robert Todd Lincoln Beckwith in personal property	$ 13,685
Alice Colonna, in cash	2,500
Mary E. Colonna Schmid, in cash	2,500

The tax return was now in the hands of the Internal Revenue Service. It would be fifteen months before the Service would render its decision.

For the next several months Campbell's work on the estate would involve only routine matters. It wasn't until July 8, 1976 that he received a phone call from Carl Rechner of the Church. Rechner wanted Campbell to set up a public meeting in Manchester. Campbell knew very well what the meeting would be about. On April 15, 1976 he had spoken to Mr. Kenngott of the Church. A day later, in a letter to his co-executor Emil Lemay, Campbell wrote of his conversation with Kenngott:

> *Kenngott said although a final decision has not been reached, it appears that the Church will probably decide to dispose of the Manchester property.*

. . . .

Meanwhile, in Manchester, Vermont, Arthur O'Dea was applying his talents as a country lawyer — gaining in reputation as each year went by. O'Dea had given up a lucrative law partnership in Northern New Jersey to move his family to Vermont in 1969. A graduate of Holy Cross College and Georgetown University Law School, O'Dea clerked with a small Arlington, Vermont law practice for six months in order to qualify for the Vermont Bar. Not long after he finished his clerkship under John L. Whalen, Esq., O'Dea set out on his own. By the mid-seventies he had opened his solo practice in Manchester.

In 1969 Manchester had only a handful of lawyers. The influx of "second home owners" to the ski areas of Bromley, Stratton and Magic Mountain were to form the basis of O'Dea's growing practice. It was his professional and personal relationship with Manchester's Town Manager, Henry R. Lambert that was to tie O'Dea to Hildene.

The thirty-year-old Henry Lambert, known locally as Hank,

was a former seminarian and congressional aide from northern Vermont. In 1976, with the town offices only a short distance from O'Dea's Center Hill Office Building, Lambert would visit with O'Dea at least twice a week to discuss town business. It was during one such visit in late spring, 1976 that he informed the town attorney of his conversation with representatives of the Church in Boston.

The Church's point man for the disposition of Hildene was Carl Rechner. The church had hired Rechner as their real estate consultant and it was he who made the original contact with Hank Lambert.

Rechner's motive for scheduling a meeting with the Town Manager at a public hearing in Manchester was to determine if, in fact, local residents had any interest in Hildene.

As noted earlier, Manchester in the Summer of 1976 was not the hub of retailing and commercial activity that it is today. The Bi-Centennial activity was one of the few points of economic optimism.

Lambert strongly believed that Hildene had to be preserved as an historic site, despite the fact that its conversion into a housing development would have made more economic and real estate tax sense to the town.

Hank Lambert informed others in Manchester of the pending arrival of the Church's delegation. Almost all of those that he had informed had a keen interest in Hildene.

On the afternoon of July 23, 1976, fifty or so Manchester residents gathered at The Town's basement meeting room to greet the representatives of the future owners of Hildene. In fact, 2% of the town's whole population was present.

Jim Campbell was correct about the size of the turnout. In his July 8, 1976 letter to Emil Lemay of Citibank, he stated:

I do not anticipate that many persons will attend the meeting, but at least the Church will have made the attempt to inform the townspeople of the reasons for their decisions.

The attentive audience first heard from someone they all knew and respected, James B. Campbell, Peggy Beckwith's attorney and the co-executor of her estate. The soft-spoken Campbell quickly and deliberately pointed out that Hildene, the 412 acres and approximately $425,000 in securities were going to the Church.

Campbell at this time had full knowledge of the fact that the six life beneficiaries of the trust set up by Peggy in her Will had all died prior to Peggy —- he was not ready to reveal it; in any event, the Church was going to get the proceeds of this trust as well as an additional sum of $425,000. Why he failed to mention this fact is not known. Three months earlier, he had filed the estate's tax return noting that the Church was to receive a sum far in excess of what was in the Will. His remarks were brief and to the point. In short order, he introduced Carl B. Rechner, the Church's consultant. Rechner was accompanied to Manchester by Glenn S. Kenngott, an attorney in the legal department of the Church. Interviews with some of those present at this first meeting concluded that there couldn't have been a greater contrast in two members of the legal profession than that of Attorney Campbell and Attorney Kenngott. The latter was more in the mold of a Wall Street investment banker and the former, the quintessential country lawyer.

In contrast to Campbell's brevity, Rechner was not brief at all. According to a report of the meeting in the July 29, 1976 Manchester

Journal, Rechner was quoted as saying:

The Christian Science Church's policy was to dispose of donated real estate at fair market value; proceeds from such sales were to be used for the advancement of religion.

The Christian Science Church had done extensive work regarding the feasibility of rehabilitating and modernizing the main house. They came to the conclusion that it was not feasible!

And thus, having come to that conclusion, their purpose in being in Manchester was to see if there was any group able to finance the purchase of the property, in its entirety, for the purpose of preserving it.

Obviously, at this time most of those in the audience began to realize that the rumors that had been circulating for months — that Hildene might be disposed of by the Church — were no longer rumors.

Rechner could see from the faces in the gathering that he had dropped a bomb. He made a veiled attempt to soften its impact by telling them that they were the first group he had spoken with. His next remark caught them all off-guard and left them almost speechless. He said,

If you are at all interested in purchasing the property, then you have ninety days to develop a plan to purchase.

After a long and silent pause, First Selectman Douglas P. Schner responded by telling Rechner that there was only a small group of Manchester citizens at the hearing and that they had never done anything like this before. He pleaded for more time. Rechner probably realized by now the impact that his bluntness must have had on the audience. He responded by saying that the Church might bend in giving more time. He added that the Church would certainly offer a liberal discount over the property's appraisal. The Church would entertain an offer for $500,000 instead of the $625,000 appraisal. He also left the impression that there were others 'out there' who had their 'eyes' on the estate and its contents. He mentioned Lincoln Memorial University as being one.

The statement he had made was momentous. Its impact was wide. Rechner's remark appeared on the front page of the July 29, 1976 *The Wall Street Journal,* as part of a larger story.

Hank Lambert at this point felt that nothing more would be gained by continuing the discussion with the Church representatives. He agreed that he would undertake the establishment of a committee that would try to find a buyer for the property. Joining with him on that committee and in attendance on that warm July afternoon were:

- Oscar V. Johnson, Jr.
- Debbie Gemmel
- Mr. & Mrs. Earl Hill
- Mrs. Joseph Fowler
- John West
- William Whitman
- David Wilson
- Ken & Lois Hill
- Selectman Schner

Lambert did not want to waste time. He called for a meeting of the volunteers that night at 7:30 at the Town Hall.

Someone also suggested that it would be wise if a trustee from the Village of Manchester also served. The reason that the group of volunteers found it necessary to extend this invitation to the Village was unknown. The Village was not given any official recognition that day. Ironically, the main house and 140 acres lay within the Village and not the Town. Speculation was that the Village trustees were indifferent as to the outcome of Hildene. Hildene's development into home sites would not be a nightmare to them, especially since the closed-up Equinox Hotel, located in the heart of the Village, loomed as a major symbol of the hard economic woes they were facing. We do not know. The invitation never went out. The Village was never represented at any of the group's subsequent meetings.

. . . .

In retrospect, the indifference displayed by the Village of Manchester in its lack of representation toward the group's concerns must have been contagious. Later that same night, only twelve people showed up to hear Hank Lambert plead with those present that "we must define our goals." This statement was his response after hearing from them that "we must preserve Hildene but we don't know how."

Others at the meeting began to speak up voicing their concerns that something had to be done. One such person was a former World War II Army pilot, Robert Thum of Dorset. A retired executive of the Cleveland stock brokerage firm of Prescott, Ball and Turbin, Thum's comments were destined to become the foundation of today's Hildene philosophy. The August 5, 1976 Manchester Journal quoted him as saying:

We have a valuable historical site and a great tourist attraction along the lines of Schuylerville and Ticonderoga in New York and the Calvin Coolidge Home in Plymouth [Vermont].

Lambert began to hand out assignments. It was time to begin work. John West was asked to contact Bruce MacDougal, the regional director of the National Trust for Historic Preservation. William Whitman agreed to do research on foundations that might provide assistance as well as list Hildene's contiguous landowners. The purpose of the latter assignment was not made known. The information was readily obtainable from the Hildene deed and survey.

The most important act of volunteerism to come out of the meeting was that of Robert C. 'Bob' Schmid. He was a former executive of the Ford Foundation and the husband of Mary Colonna Schmid, a distant cousin and close friend of Peggy Beckwith. He offered to write up the overall objectives of what he perceived to be the group's purpose. That same evening Bob christened the group by proposing to those present the name, 'Friends of Hildene'.

Lambert felt it was important to get on with the business of the Friends of Hildene. He asked that others be called on to help, regardless of whether they were from Manchester or not. His vision was that Hildene open itself to a much larger audience. The Friends of Hildene's efforts in preserving the estate needed to reach beyond the local town and village. He called for a third meeting to be held on August 12th in order to review the work which was now about to begin.

• •

The work to be accomplished before the meeting of the 12th of August was interrupted by an unscheduled guest to the area —

Hurricane Belle. Manchester was hit hard. Flooding was everywhere, especially in front of Oscar Johnson's farm where the placid Battenkill River became a raging torrent.

Despite the storm and its damage to his constituents' property, Hank Lambert would not be swayed from his goal of moving the Friends of Hildene forward. He was excited to have received on August 10, 1976, a letter from Alice B. Colonna of Woodbridge, Connecticut. Ms. Colonna was a distant cousin of Peggy's. Alice and her brother-in-law's wife, Mary E. Colanna Schmid, were the daughters of Frances Isham Colonna and through marriage, connected to Peggy's aunt. She wrote to Lambert to inform him that she had mentioned to Attorney Campbell her cousin's intentions, as she had known them.

Peggy, according to Ms. Colonna, had wanted to make parts of Hildene into a self-sufficient dairy farm and to lease to Burr & Burton (the local high school) the north farmhouse. Alice went on to tell Lambert that she regretted not being able to attend the meeting set for August 23rd, but that she would help the Friends of Hildene.

The group reconvened on August 12, 1976 and Lambert made two profound announcements. One was that Attorney O'Dea would move immediately to file for a tax exempt status for the Friends of Hildene. The other one was that the Church had informed him that they would entertain taking a long term mortgage from a purchaser.

That night Lambert did not mention to the group that the Church had not wavered on their ninety-day deadline. The Friends of Hildene were already all too well aware of its significance.

But only O'Dea knew what was involved in filing with the Internal Revenue Service for exempt status. His years of practicing law had grounded him in the intricacies of working through section

501(c)(3) of the Federal Tax Code. He also knew that more than simple approval under section 501 for the 'Friends of Hildene' was needed to avoid taxation. It was imperative that monies contributed to the 'Friends of Hildene' be considered charitable contributions by the donors under Section 170 of the Code. Otherwise, it would be futile to go out and seek funds if the donors would not be able to obtain a tax deduction.

The nuances of the Code were the least of O'Dea's concerns. Who would file? He needed an entity and there was none in existence in early August of 1976. He was also well aware of the time it would take for a group of volunteers to adopt the Articles of Association and accompanying By-Laws. It would not be easy for this new loosely formed group to quickly (1) define the terms of office for trustees, (2) select officers and (3) define the group's basic purpose.

Lambert and Schmid shared O'Dea's concerns. Schmid, in fact, had experience in the area of creating a non-profit entity. Shortly after the meeting of the 12th, O'Dea met with Schmid and Lambert and it was decided that they must move swiftly to form a corporation, elect a board of trustees and appoint officers who could act on behalf of the corporation. They were also well aware of the fact that some members of the founding group were much closer to Hildene than they were. All three of them were 'outsiders'. They knew that no matter how well intentioned their motives, it was critical that they bring into their circle someone who was more closely linked to Peggy and Hildene than they were. They needed a consensus builder. This remarkable individual was Oscar V. Johnson, Jr.

Oscar Johnson was sixty-four, a retired heating oil company president, a farmer and a quintessential local volunteer. His efforts were essential in mapping out a strategy to get the Friends of Hildene formally organized. This had to be accomplished without stepping on toes. He had to avoid all of the potential delays found in the endless discussions of By-Laws and procedures that normally accompany such endeavors. Schmid and O'Dea were very careful not to alienate any of those in the group whose assistance was going to be needed, so that the October 20th deadline with the Church could be met.

It was now time to move simultaneously on many fronts. Lambert called for an organization meeting to be held on August 23, 1976. O'Dea prepared the Articles of Association. Schmid and Johnson signed them on August 19, 1976. Within one day, August 20, 1976, the Vermont Secretary of State gave the Friends of Hildene its Certificate of Incorporation.

· ·

Exactly one year to the day that Peggy Beckwith's Will was probated — August 23, 1976 — an Organizational Meeting of the Friends of Hildene was held at 7:30 in the evening at Manchester's Town Hall. Hank Lambert opened the meeting by reading the Articles of Association to the twenty-five original members out of a list of eighty who were present. It was obvious to everyone present that Lambert wanted Friends of Hildene to be made official. It was not so obvious that he personally felt uncomfortable in his dual role — town manager and his unofficial role of spearheading the drive to save Hildene. It was a challenge he surely knew would haunt him in any dispute brought by the new owners of the property, potential purchasers and others in the Town who were not in favor of turning Hildene into a historical site and removing it from the tax rolls.

Lambert pressed on. He asked for the slate of nominees for

trustees. Before he accepted the slate he read the duties. He also spoke on what the trustees could contribute. He was looking for nine nominees. He got the following from the members present:

- Ken Hill
- Susan Hill
- Oscar Johnson, Jr.
- Romi Perkins
- William Whitman
- Carl Saladino
- Robert Schmid
- Robert Thum
- John West

Surprisingly, Art O'Dea did not stand for election. He did agree to stay involved as the attorney for the Friends of Hildene, at no charge. Within a year he would be Vice Chairman of the Board.

Lambert's last act as the meeting's chair was to ask that the newly formed Board elect a slate of officers. Oscar Johnson nominated Bob Schmid to be President and Chairman of the Board. Thum was elected as Treasurer and Susan Hill as Secretary. Johnson was elected Vice President. The Board and its officers were in place. The business of Hildene could now move forward. The Board would have eleven meetings before 1976 was over.

Hank Lambert stepped aside. He passed the gavel on to Bob Schmid and went back to being Manchester's Town Manager for all of the people. Nevertheless, Lambert's vision, initiative, and guidance were so critical in the founding of the Friends of Hildene that, because of his actions in the Spring and Summer of 1976, Hildene was saved. A few years later he moved to Montpelier and began to apply his skills in State government.

· ·

With the formal procedures now out of the way, Schmid lost no time in assuming the leadership role. He, more than anyone, knew how overwhelming the tasks in front of them were. He also knew well about the scarcity of their resources with regard to time, money and management skills.

Bob Schmid, who only months before turned sixty years old, was the ideal person to have been selected chairman of this embryonic group. He was studious, detailed, and creative. He was a no-nonsense person with one purpose — to save Hildene!

His career as a project manager and Vice President with the Ford Foundation in New York City spanned twenty years. This work was proceeded by his five years helping to rebuild Europe after World War II when he was assigned to the Marshall Plan. Neither his doctorate from the University of Wisconsin in Sociology nor his Bachelor's degree from Ohio University appeared to be the correct credentials for someone who was so involved with the United States Government's spy operations, the OSS. This organization was the predecessor to the CIA and existed from 1943 to the end of the War. He was professional, intelligent, and persuasive. It was time for him to go to work again — for a new cause.

Despite his election only moments before, Schmid had his agenda ready to go. He did not want to be distracted. When Bob Thum made a motion for the adoption of a detailed list of Committee assignments, Schmid cut him off, ever so diplomatically. Schmid wanted the concentration of the Organization focused on four areas: fundraising, publicity/communication, historical research and, most importantly, updating the feasibility study. The latter was necessary because, in Schmid's mind, $500,000 would need to be raised if the Friends of

Hildene were to acquire the property.

Schmid was well aware of the contribution Bob Thum could make to their undertaking. Thum, who only a few months earlier had moved to Dorset, Vermont from Cleveland, had retired as an executive with the Cleveland stock brokerage firm of Prescott, Ball and Tumbull. Thum had known from the outset that they were going to have difficult negotiations with the Church. He was not afraid of this. After all, he was a decorated Air Corps aviator in the Pacific during World War II.

Schmid specifically asked Attorney O'Dea to search for any legal ground on which they could rely that might stretch out the Church's deadline. Schmid would later learn that O'Dea had already begun his research. Schmid noted that he and his wife, Mary, would contact Robert Lincoln 'Bud' Beckwith and find out if he would be willing to make a large contribution to their cause. He assigned the task of inspecting and inventorying all of the physical property items to Oscar Johnson and Ken Hill. This assignment was most logical, as both men were quite familiar with the property. Not all assignments had to be given out by Schmid. Bob Thum said at the meeting that he and his wife, Millie, together with Mary and Ed Bort, noted local historians, would do the necessary research on the history of Hildene. Oscar volunteered to call the Church the next day and let them know that the Friends of Hildene were now functioning.

Not unlike many other Vermont meetings of volunteers of citizens' groups, everyone felt that he or she could join in the discussion at almost any time or place. This practice made the formality Schmid sought disintegrate. Lambert jumped in to note that in his most recent conversation with the Church they were holding to their ninety-day schedule. Even the quiet and reserved Ken Hill spoke up to tell those present that his impression was that the Church was bluffing. He conveyed to the group his conversation with the estate attorney, Jim Campbell. The co-executor had informed Ken that the Church was not about to receive any property as a distribution from the estate until some time in the following year.

Although somewhat impatient regarding the meeting's digression from his agenda, Schmid felt that Hill's announcement, if right, was crucial information. How could the Church convey something to which they did not hold title?

It was after 9:30 PM, the meeting was heading into its third hour. It was late for many of those present. Schmid knew this and yet he wanted to refocus the group's attention to the feasibility study. It was his belief that any fundraising would be futile in the absence of this study. The question then became: who was capable of doing one? Schmid noted that he would contact people at the National Trust for Historic Preservation as well as people at the University of Vermont. It was his conclusion that they would be able to assist the Friends of Hildene in the area of financial feasibility.

It was now 9:50 PM. Schmid asked for a motion to adjourn, but only after telling everyone that there would be another meeting the next day.

. . . .

A month had now passed since Mr. Rechner of the Church had been in Manchester. There were less than sixty days left to come up with a proposal to purchase the property.

After the organizational meeting had adjourned, Schmid was made aware of a tactic Attorney O'Dea had been quietly working on. It was one which O'Dea did not want to make public. Earlier that

Summer, after O'Dea had reviewed Peggy's Will and the Church's intentions with Hank Lambert, he had swung into action. He believed that there must be some legal precedent that he could use to prevent the Church from executing a sale without first attempting to carry out the wishes of Peggy. In reading Peggy's Will, all four-and-a-half pages, O'Dea riveted on two important statements Peggy had made. The first one, contained in the Will's sixth clause stated, in part, that:

> ... *it being my direction that said Hildene estate shall be a memorial to my mother and grandparents.*

O'Dea understood the importance of this clause. So did the Friends of Hildene, for whom it was the primary basis of their motivation. But to O'Dea it was not sufficient grounds. There must be more. And, sure enough, there was. It was contained in one word, deep within the seventh clause:

> ... *In the event that at any time said Board of Directors [of the Christian Science Church] shall determine that it is* **impractical** *to keep and maintain said Hildene estate as a memorial, I authorize and empower them to sell any part and all of said real estate ... at a public or private sale.*

The word "impractical" was the lightning rod that would provide the source of energy to O'Dea. Once he knew Peggy's specific wishes, he felt that it was imperative that he undertake research into case law on the issue of whether the Church could, in fact, sell the property without first attempting to determine the practicality of maintaining Hildene as a memorial.

O'Dea, like many other country attorneys, worked as a sole practitioner. He would often engage legal research firms to do extensive work that involved unusual issues.

One such firm was The Research Group, Inc. of Boston. This firm, utilized in other cases by O'Dea, would engage the services of Harvard Law School professors and students. O'Dea authorized them to do the research, urging them to conduct it speedily and for no more than $500. The Research Group acted on O'Dea's wishes.

On August 24, 1976, O'Dea received from Roger Singer of the Research Group, Inc. a thirteen-page brief that would later prove invaluable. He told Schmid the news. However, it was the news that Schmid conveyed to O'Dea that was even more startling and invaluable.

Ken Hill, the quiet, unassuming and dutiful caretaker of Hildene since 1947, informed Schmid that an anonymous donor had agreed to give the Friends of Hildene two hundred thousand dollars toward the purchase of Hildene. Schmid, O'Dea, and shortly thereafter, their officers and trustees, were dumbfounded. They felt that everything that they had done to date was important and necessary but, in the absence of any source of funds, they were not going to play any significant role in the acquisition. The late evening call that Ken Hill had received from the anonymous donor would change the strategy of the Friends of Hildene. The pledge had to be confirmed in writing. The donor's terms had to be noted and agreed to. And, most importantly, the gift had to be specifically earmarked toward the purchase of the property. It had to be tax deductible and, if not used within two years, it would be forfeited.

Reality soon came back to the pragmatic Schmid and O'Dea. The filing with the IRS to become a tax exempt organization took on greater importance and immediacy. And, although $200,000 was a long way from the $500,000 sales price, the two knew that they had a start.

. . . .

The period between the Organizational Meeting of August 23, 1976 and September 15, 1976 saw a flurry of activity.

O'Dea, together with Schmid, worked at drafting the material required to file for tax exempt status. One document that was to be part of the filing was the Friends of Hildene By-Laws. The two professionals were well aware that this should not be some perfunctory document. It had to be thought out. Its drafting took on conflicting objectives. Because Hildene was to be a non-profit corporation, it was not capable of selling stock. Instead, for fundraising purposes, it was going to sell memberships on a national basis. Members in a non-profit organization then became the "owners" and could vote. Schmid's and O'Dea's concern was that if they and their colleagues were successful in acquiring Hildene, it might be possible for a group of members to emerge and undo all that they had done. The greatest fear, of course, would be that such a group might not embrace the founders' goals. They might want to sell off part of the property.

Legally, this was prevented by structuring the By-Laws for the election of trustees, term limits and meetings. The document was finally drafted. On September 10, 1976, the request from the IRS for tax exempt status was filed.

While O'Dea and others were carrying out their assignments, Schmid followed up on his task regarding contacting Robert Lincoln

Beckwith. He was successful in garnering the support of the great grandson of Abraham Lincoln — both in modest financial terms and in spirit. Beckwith, who had a great fondness for Hildene, accepted the invitation to become the Honorary Chairman of the Board of Trustees on September 10, 1976. It was a coup for Schmid in that the Friends of Hildene now had a nationally recognized name upon which to go out and do fundraising. From Beckwith's standpoint, he felt that the Friends of Hildene was the right group to preserve his late sister's home. He had spent many calming weeks at Hildene, particularly a decade before, when his personal life was coming apart due to a terribly upsetting and litigious divorce.

· ·

The history of the period surrounding the formation of the Friends of Hildene and what followed shortly thereafter is well documented. What is not so well known and even less well documented are the motives behind those that made it happen. There may have been the common motive of a sense of history that needed to be preserved. For some it might have been the fact that Hildene and its property could be lost to developers. Surely, contiguous neighbors felt a need for preservation of their own property. Certainly this could be said about Oscar Johnson and Robert Schmid. One might also have been motivated by the personal and professional exhilaration of being involved with such a highly respected group bent on carrying out such a lofty quest. And, to others who knew Peggy so well, it might have been that they felt she was reaching out to them to protect Hildene and preserve it for generations to come as the memorial to her mother and grandparents as she requested in her Will.

It was in early September 1976, that Schmid and O'Dea agreed that it was time to go to Boston and meet with the Church. The struggle to acquire Hildene was about to really begin.

View of Hildene's center hall and dining room in July 1975.

Hildene's guest room in 1975, now showcase of Peggy's hobbies.

Beula C. Nunn, wife of former Governor of Kentucky in attic of Hildene, February, 1976 – searching for treasures to return them to Kentucky.

Nunn's photograph of silver brush set which she later received as a
gift from Robert Lincoln Beckwith.

Hildene's south view prior to 1975.

Early in the morning, on the second Monday in September, 1976, Bob Schmid picked up Attorney O'Dea at O'Dea's Center Hill Office Building.

In contrast to O'Dea's three-piece suit, Schmid dressed like a college professor. His somewhat disheveled appearance coordinated well with his twelve-year-old Checker cab that was ready to take them to Boston to meet with officers of the Church. On this particular occasion O'Dea, who had always enjoyed Bob Schmid's company, had wished that he were home in bed. He felt miserable. His malaise was, in part, due to a late summer cold. It was made worse by his withdrawal from caffeine, which he had begun the Friday before.

Nevertheless, the four-hour journey was marked by non-stop conversations about the mission they had embarked upon. And despite his physical condition O'Dea was excited and so was Schmid. They had no idea how they would be received by the Church or who, in addition to Carl Rechner, would be at the meeting. O'Dea knew that the Church had its own legal staff and certainly someone with legal training would be with Rechner. The Church was also represented by several of Boston's oldest and most prestigious law firms. O'Dea wondered if they would also be at the meeting. His portfolio was, at best, thin. Armed only with the pledge of a $200,000 gift, a legal brief and the Friends of Hildene charter, O'Dea knew that he and Schmid were going into uncharted waters.

Bob Schmid, the recently elected Chairman of the Board, used the time it took to get to Boston going over their strategy with O'Dea time and again. It was nearly a year from the time that he and his wife, Mary, had written to Attorney Campbell expressing their interest in saving Hildene. It was nearly seven years from the date that he and Mary were summoned to the 'Big House' by Cousin Peg to sit in on a meeting regarding an earlier potential disposition of Hildene. Had such a disposition gone to fruition, the trip he was now on would not have been necessary.

In the late 1960s Peggy had a meeting with a Mr. Bradford of the Nature Conservancy as well as with Captain Kotrala of Trout Unlimited. The purpose of that meeting was to find an organization that would take responsibility for the house; Peggy was nearly seventy years old at the time of the meeting. Kotrala suggested that one wing of the house be a trout-fishing museum and that the other wing be an Abraham Lincoln museum. One part of the property borders the Battenkill River. Trout Unlimited's huge endowment led Kotrala to come up with the scheme. Peggy's attorney James Campbell also attended the meeting but said little. Later that day Patrick Noonan, a friend of Robert Beckwith and a Director of Operations in the Nature Conservancy, called Schmid and told him that he thought the meeting had gone well. That might very well have been the case. However, the next day Peggy called off the whole idea. She did not want to divide the property nor did she want it used as a memorial to Abraham Lincoln. Instead, she wanted it as a memorial to her mother and grandparents.

As he drove his Checker down I-91 toward Massachusetts' Route 2, Schmid's thoughts came back to 1976. He was not going to allow Hildene to be negotiated away, to be utilized for some other purpose.

. . . .

O'Dea and Schmid were speechless when they looked up from the curb at the glass skyscraper that housed the Church's world headquarters. They had not expected this. There was more to come. A handsome young boy wearing a yellow blazer with a Christian Science Church identification badge clearly spelling out his name and position, told them, ever so politely, to use the underground parking facility. Walking from the garage to the elevators, they were met by another youngster with neatly combed hair and an air of country freshness about him. He would be their escort to the inner sanctum of the Church headquarters. The sudden opening of the elevator doors on the upper-most floor of the building was the event that signaled to O'Dea and Schmid that they had arrived. They were now big league players and there would no retreating now, not with Rechner's office only a few yards away.

· ·

Carl Rechner sat behind a very large oak desk. On his left was Philip Hunt, Associate Counsel to the Church, and on his right sat his attorney, Glenn Kenngott. The General Counsel for the Church, John R. Peterson, was not present. Peterson was one of two attorneys on the legal staff of the Church in September of 1949 when Arthur W. Eckman, then General Counsel, wrote to Jim Campbell, Peggy's attorney, to thank him for informing the Church that they were to be the named beneficiary of Peggy's Will.

A panoramic view of the city of Boston was visible through the large window directly behind Rechner's desk. O'Dea recalls vividly how Rechner welcomed them in a 'heavenly way'. Rechner's voice was clear but soft. Moments later, however, the conversation went from the divine to dollars! And despite all of the trappings and appearances of being at the headquarters of a religious institution, O'Dea came to his senses and realized that this meeting was about real estate. How much were the Friends of Hildene willing to pay to purchase a property the Church was about to own?

Schmid informed the attorneys for the Church about the formation of the Friends of Hildene. He also told them about the anonymous gift, but did not disclose the amount. They smiled ever so politely, acknowledging his remarks. They were not totally impressed. The visitors did not have a counter to their price of $500,000. Schmid was not ready to counter at this time. It was too early in the meeting. He wanted his colleague to introduce his findings obtained through his legal research. He was establishing their position.

O'Dea, in a matter-of-fact way, told the three Church representatives about his findings. Rechner responded by saying that they had done research as well. And it was their opinion that the Church was well within its rights to move on the sale of the property in the event that the Friends of Hildene did not meet the deadline. The discussion quickly became litigious, as could be expected with three attorneys being in the same room.

O'Dea told them that litigation would not be in the Church's best interest, especially with the publicity that would attend any courtroom action.

"Imagine," O'Dea told them, "what would your potential testators think if they knew that you do not abide by the wishes of a Will?"

O'Dea went on to tell them.

56

"Even if the Church won the legal fight, they would lose,"

There was dead silence — it was like an eternity. O'Dea broke the silence by adding that

> *"If the issue did for some reason go to trial, it would be in Vermont, in the Northshire courthouse across from the Equinox and half a mile from Hildene, and heard before a Vermont judge and two side judges."*

Rechner's response to O'Dea's legal scenario was completely unexpected. He dropped the Church's latest price for Hildene from $500,000 to $400,000. In doing so, Attorney Hunt would later state that

> *"It was motivated by altruism rather than by any doubt as to Miss Beckwith's wishes."*

Hunt also noted that Rechner had done this in recognition of the issues O'Dea had raised.

O'Dea and Schmid did not know what to say. A recess was asked for. O'Dea and Schmid went into another room. How long their caucus lasted and what was discussed are not known. What is known, however, is that the two Vermonters went back to the meeting. They offered the Church $165,000 for the property and all of its contents.

The Church wanted time to review, not only the offer, but also O'Dea's legal research. The meeting ended cordially and coolly. O'Dea and Schmid left for Vermont. They had fired their first salvos. They thought they were in the game, at least for now.

. . . .

The trip back to Vermont was a nightmare for O'Dea. He thought he was dying. His withdrawal from coffee was taking its toll on him. Schmid was not fully aware of what was wrong. Somewhere on the trip back O'Dea asked Schmid to pull the car off the road. O'Dea became violently ill. Slightly embarrassed, O'Dea wondered what this former executive of the Ford Foundation was possibly thinking about him. At that moment, he felt weak and sick, not the strong attorney, the defender of Hildene. Bob Schmid had the only thought that he could have — we are all human. He helped O'Dea back into the car and made him as comfortable as possible. He knew quite well that if the Friends of Hildene were to ever close the gap between $165,000 and $400,000 he was going to need this friend.

· ·

Robert and Mary Schmid's home, Rocking Stone Farm, was situated on the westerly side of Route 7 (now 7A). The house was set up on a gentle slope, providing the Schmids beautiful views of both Edward Swift Isham's home, Ormsby Hill, and beyond it, Hildene. It was now autumn, midway through the second Fall since Mary's cousin had died. The study in the Farm gave Bob the privacy to do the planning that needed to be done to save Hildene. He knew that the Friends of Hildene were a well- meaning, hard working and dedicated group, but they were not wealthy. He knew that it was going to take hundreds of thousands of dollars to acquire, restore and maintain Hildene, if they were successful. The anonymous donor's gift would just not be enough — nor would belligerence, he thought, as manifested in O'Dea's legal brief.

However, on October 16th, he was encouraged by a phone call he received from O'Dea, during which he learned that the IRS had approved the Friends of Hildene tax exempt status — less than a month and a half from when it was filed. The IRS informed the Friends of Hildene that not only would the Friends of Hildene's income not be taxed but, more importantly, the donations they would obtain could be considered "tax deductible" by the donors. The attorney for the anonymous donor had to be informed immediately.

However, the good news would not last long. On November 2, 1976 Phil Hunt, the attorney for the Christian Science Church, informed O'Dea that the legal brief presented by O'Dea had been rejected. He also stated that the $400,000 price was fixed, thereby rejecting the Friends of Hildene's $165,000 offer. Even more critical was the fact that the ninety-day time period for the Friends of Hildene to come up with a plan had expired. The Church in its own opinion was now free to offer the property to others.

Bob Schmid was talented, and a creative thinker. He knew that obtaining more money was going to be the solution. He informed his executive committee about the need to solicit support from other non-profits, particularly foundations, about the need to create a national membership organization and about the need to hire a professional fundraiser.

He had some success with the first and second ideas. The Eva Gebhard-Gourgaud Foundation was instrumental in giving Hildene their support in the form of a two-thousand-dollar donation. In addition, they offered advice about hiring an archivist to inventory, appraise and to best utilize Robert Todd Lincoln's possessions for future public viewing.

Schmid did not totally embrace the idea of bringing in professional fundraisers. If he wasn't already deeply worried about the possibility of Hildene slipping away, then the Probate Court's action of November 12, 1976 delivered to him a frightening wake-up call. The Court authorized the first partial distribution. Bob's wife, Mary, together with her sister, Alice Colonna, each received their legacy of $2500. Robert Todd Lincoln Beckwith received $13,685 in the appraised value of certain personal property. Later it would turn out that Beckwith had not received all of the personal items that he was entitled to receive. It would form the basis of further delay and almost cause the failure of the Friends of Hildene to obtain Hildene.

The actions on the part of the estate's co-executors forced Schmid to act. He recommended to his executive committee the firm of Ketchum, Inc. of New York City. Schmid was referred to the firm by one of the founder's sons, Richard Ketchum, editor of The Blair and Ketchum Country Journal of Brattleboro, Vermont. Richard and wife, Barbara, lived nearby, in Dorset, Vermont.

The firm's representatives came to Manchester in late November of 1976 and met with the Friends of Hildene. In December they issued a report to O'Dea. Their credentials were impeccable. This was evident from their excellent multi-page report. The firm's ancestors had settled in Vermont fourteen generations ago. They listed as clients: art museums, historic homes, colleges and universities. One of these universities was the Lincoln Memorial University, which exceeded their fundraising goal by $1,000,000 in 1975. The firm was founded in 1919. They were the ones who could raise the $500,000 the Friends of Hildene required. They recommended the following actions:

1) continue negotiations with the Church;
2) create a newsletter;

3) finalize any open IRS issues;

4) create a list of renovations;

5) place people on the Board of Trustees who were of affluence and influence;

6) retain Ketchum;

7) have a resident consultant from the Ketchum firm in Manchester for three months.

The firm's fees probably seemed high to the Friends of Hildene (except to Schmid). Ketchum wanted $19,500 plus between $5,000 to $7,500 for operating expenses. They informed the Friends of Hildene that $3,250 of said fee must be paid the day their representative arrived in Manchester. The representative never arrived. Vermonters are not well known for making snap decisions, however in the Spring of 1977, the Board of Trustees rejected the Ketchum proposal. This ultimate decision by his fellow board members did not sit well with Schmid. They needed to do something, and do it soon. Time had almost run out — and so had their funds.

PART IV — THE DARKEST HOURS

On September 20, 1949, Arthur W. Eckman, General Counsel for the Christian Science Church, wrote to James Campbell. His purpose in writing to the Manchester attorney was to thank him for his letter of September 14, 1949 wherein Campbell informed the Church of Peggy's wishes regarding the Church being named the beneficiary of her Will. Eckman went on in his letter to state:

"And to assure you that we will extend every possible cooperation to aid in carrying out her fine purpose."

Peggy executed her Will on September 5, 1950. Twenty-seven years later, Eckman's successors were finding it impossible to carry out Peggy's wishes. The Church sued the Attorney General of Vermont as well as Robert L. Beckwith, naming them in an action for Summary Judgment, filed in Bennington County's Superior Court in April of 1977. The Church, impatient with the Friends of Hildene and Robert Todd Lincoln Beckwith, wanted to freely exercise its rights under the Will. It hired the Brattleboro law firm of Fitts and Olson to bring the action. The Friends of Hildene were not a party to the suit. Under Vermont law, the Attorney General represents the interests of the maker of the Will when there are issues concerning philanthropic trusts.

The Church was truly frustrated by this time. Philip W. Hunt, the Church's associate counsel, had written to O'Dea two months prior. In his February 18, 1977 letter to O'Dea, Hunt informed O'Dea that the Church would accept $350,000 for the property and all of its contents. He made it clear he was not willing to take $300,000. Hunt was reducing the price by $50,000 from that which was offered at their September meeting. He also presented a stick as well as the olive branch. He informed O'Dea that the Church had hired the Fitts and Olson firm. They were prepared to go forward with appropriate legal action and therefore have the court determine the issue of practicality. Patience was no longer a major part of the strategy for the Church's legal department. Hunt went on to state:

> *"If this issue is eventually resolved in our favor as we expect, the opportunity to acquire Hildene would probably be opened up to a broader spectrum of interested buyers or investors than it is now."*

The Church was determined to move swiftly. It did not want to operate the property as a museum. It was also well aware that many thousands of dollars were required to provide simply the basics of estate maintenance. A second distribution by the Probate Court was only two months away.

In a letter dated April 27, 1977, Campbell informed his co-executor, Emil Lemay, of the dealings and most recent correspondence from the Church to the Friends of Hildene. Campbell went on to note that the "Friends" was not an interested party in the probate action and that under Vermont law they could not participate. He concluded by informing Lemay that:

> *"... in my opinion the "Friends" organization is attempting to drive down the price with the threat of litigation."*

. . . .

The optimism and enthusiasm that was so evident whenever the Friends of Hildene met in their first eight months of existence was rapidly dissipating. Their April 1977 meeting brought to the surface issues that seemed insurmountable to this highly motivated group. Their cohesiveness and single-minded purpose — the saving of Hildene — was slipping away.

The initial distribution of the estate to the heirs had already taken place. The burden of an untenable purchase price from the Church as well as the lawsuit was becoming very heavy to this volunteer group of well-intentioned individuals. And, to add to their troubles, there were the rumblings out of Virginia from Robert Lincoln Beckwith, that certain of the possessions left to him by his sister were not to be found. Beckwith, who had already accepted the position of Honorary Chairman of the Friends of Hildene, was holding the organization responsible for the missing items.

Despair had set in among the Friends of Hildene. Bob Schmid asked his fellow trustees to come up with ideas, no matter how radical. And Susan Hill, the Board's secretary, was asked to collect them and bring them to the next meeting.

After the April 1977 meeting, Schmid was not ready to reconvene his board. In the last five months of the prior year he held nine meetings with his colleagues. He was not to call for another meeting until August 10, 1977, four months away. He needed time to evaluate the responses he had requested. He too was reeling from the news of the lawsuit and the impending transfer of the property to the Church.

Some of Schmid's advisors suggested that he consider turning Hildene into an agricultural college or a farm devoted to Morgan horses. Some advised using the property to display workings of functional, renewable energy sources such as wind, water and solar. He thought his trustee's ideas had drifted away from their primary mission. Other advisors suggested converting the grounds into a vocational college, an experimental farm, or a sugar house operation.

These suggestions were not very specific, however, some others were well thought out. One such idea called for developing a new company, the Hildene Land Trust Co., Inc. It would seek to attract fourteen investors who would put up $25,000 each, preferably from local people of the highest character. They would combine these funds with the $200,000 from the anonymous donor and acquire the property. Once the property was acquired it would be split up. The main house, access road and immediate grounds would be donated to the Friends of Hildene forming a sanctuary and thereby meet the requirements of the anonymous donor. The balance of the property, the wetlands along the Battenkill, would be sold to parties interested in preserving the marshes and river area and, this plan would also raise needed money. It was the next property disposition that would cause the greatest concern — the sale of property along River Road and on the high ground as building lots. The uninterrupted views from Hildene's gardens would be gone.

Bob Schmid knew his colleagues shared his concern that they were losing the struggle to save Hildene. Up until the time he had received these suggestions on how they would change course, he had not realized how desperate their thinking had become. This man of action felt it was time to take no action. It was a time to let both internal and external events run their course. He was going to wait and he did, for four months. He knew it was a gamble but he felt he had no choice if Hildene was to be preserved in one piece.

Although Schmid did not share with the full membership of Hildene exactly what was handed to him from his trustees, he did let them know how desperate things had become with the Church. He did so in the April 1977 <u>News from Friends of Hildene</u>.

> *Negotiations with Friends of Hildene at impasse as Christian Science Church seeks Court interpretation of key provisions in Mary Lincoln Beckwith's Will.*

He did not mince words. He wanted the members to know where they stood. He told them:

> *... the Church has not shown — and has made no good faith effort to establish — that to run Hildene as directed in the Will would be 'impractical.'...*

Schmid went on in the newsletter to present the legal case of the Friends of Hildene. He noted that Ms. Beckwith had wanted the Church to run Hildene as a memorial — why else, he noted, would she have given $425,000 as an endowment.

One interesting point regarding Schmid's last comment was that as late as April 1977, he was unaware that the other named heirs in Peggy's Will had predeceased her. Accordingly, the residuary estate going to the Church would be increased by another $425,000. All one can conclude is that he and his colleagues would have been even more incensed.

. . . .

Robert Lincoln (Bud) Beckwith was hopeful that 1977 would bring some happiness into his life. Yet, in the Spring of 1977, the three times married "last of the Lincolns" was still grieving over the loss of his sister Peggy and suffering from acute Parkinson's disease. But, the one thing that had taken greater toll on him physically, mentally and financially was the recently ended paternity trial with his second wife, Annemarie Hoffman Beckwith.

The trial, which was held in the U.S. District Court Washington, D.C., had gained national attention. The reason for this attention was not only because the plaintiff was a Lincoln descendent, but also because of the issues of desertion, money and the sensational question — Did, in fact, Robert father a child with Annemarie? After weeks of testimony it was decided that Robert was sterile. The child, who would be approximately thirty-three years old in 2001, was determined not to have been Robert's son.

The distraction of going to Vermont to sort through his late sister's possessions at Hildene was a welcomed relief for him. He was glad he had James Hickey with him.

On April 19, 1977 he arrived in Manchester. His usual companion was Margaret Fristoe. She would become his wife later in the year. However, this time she was not with him. Nevertheless, she was quite pleased that Jim Hickey's wife, Betty, had gone along with him because she would see to it that he would take his medicine. They would be at Hildene until April 25. According to Jim Hickey, it had been a difficult week working with Bud. Hickey needed him to identify certain items that belonged to his sister. Bud would only stay at the house for a few hours each morning. Then, after eating a lunch that had been prepared by Betty, he would want go back to his room at the

Colburn House (now the Northshire Bookstore). He was sometimes physically and emotionally exhausted.

Their mission would quickly become so upsetting that it would motivate Robert Lincoln Beckwith to ask to have his name removed as Honorary Chairman of the Board of Trustees of Hildene.

To place Robert Beckwith's consternation and frustration in perspective one must realize the large magnitude of the work involved in evaluating all of the personal property and possessions.

In addition to the dozens of trunks, most of which were stored in Hildene's attic, there were over one hundred boxes containing papers, artifacts and mementos belonging to almost every one of the Lincolns.

Before Beckwith and Hickey had the opportunity to evaluate the contents of the boxes and the trunks or the many items of furniture and furnishings, some other people had been at work. Mrs. Nunn from Kentucky and other appraisers studied many items. Attorney Campbell had also been involved as well as his co-executor, Lemay, and Phil Hunt of the Church.

Campbell was not unaware of the pressure being brought by the Friends of Hildene to keep the possessions intact and secured. On May 17, 1977, in a letter to Elizabeth Young, Robert Beckwith's attorney, he noted:

> " I do not expect any real difficulty with the Church, but 'The Friends of Hildene' are looking for everything they can lay their hands on if they are able to arrive at a purchase and sales agreement of Hildene with the Church ..."

Campbell, as co-executor, was being placed under enormous pressure from all sides. In spite of such pressure, he did not yield in carrying out his duties. In the same letter to Miss Young, he informed her that James Hickey and Robert Beckwith had recently been at Hildene. They sorted through the items that had been given to Beckwith and boxed them. Those boxes were now awaiting shipment to Wilson's Storage in Rutland, Vermont. Campbell told Young that before the boxes left Hildene he would personally inventory them to be certain that the boxes contained only those items noted in Article Second and Seventh of Peggy's Will.

There was, however, one item that was noted in Article Seven of the Will that was to go to Robert but could not be found. That item was the bronze sculpture of Abraham Lincoln's hands cast from life. It was made in the 1860s by the sculptor Leonard Volk. He made castings from both of Abraham Lincoln's hands. The fact that the bronze hands could not be found among the estate's possessions did not fare well with Robert Beckwith or James Hickey. The sculpture was supposed to have been at Hildene but was gone.

To understand why the bronze hands were not at Hildene, one must go back to May 14, 1960 and to the U.S. Naval Base, Portsmouth, New Hampshire. On that particular day Peggy christened the USS Abraham Lincoln (SSB(N)602), a nuclear ballistic missile submarine. She was accompanied by Ken and Lois Hill, together with others from her Hildene staff — Roger Wilcox, John and Norma Thompson. According to Ken Hill, it was a special day for Peggy. She got all dressed up — a rare event. Many patriotic Americans watched her as she broke the bottle of champagne against the boat's hull.

Later, to show her gratitude and appreciation to the Navy, she turned over the bronze sculptured hands of her great grandfather. And, about a year later on April 10, 1961, after the vessel had been completed, she received a letter from the submarine's Captain, L. Erb. He told Peggy that the 'hands' had been mounted on the boat's passageway between the control center and the enlisted men's living quarters. Captain Erb thanked her by sending a picture of the submarine at sea.

The question of where the 'hands' went remained an unsolved mystery for many years. James Campbell could have told them, had he been aware of Captain Erb's letter filed away in his client's folder. It wasn't until the preparations were underway for the commissioning of the USS Abraham Lincoln CVN 72 nuclear aircraft carrier in 1989, that James Hickey finally realized what had happened to the hands. In his work with the Illinois Commissioning Committee he came upon Captain Erb's letter.

Robert Schmid recalled Bud Beckwith's serious concern about the missing item. It was becoming a major problem, a major disturbance to all. Trust was fading quickly, especially so when James Campbell and then Robert Lincoln Beckwith began to hear rumors that items belonging to Beckwith were showing up at yard sales and auctions throughout Bennington County.

Such events did not surprise Schmid. He was quite familiar with Peggy's practice of giving her possessions to close friends and to people who had worked on the estate - perhaps forgetting that she had already Willed those items to other people or places.

There was not much James Campbell could do. He persisted in having the Church come to Manchester and sign off on the possessions they were to receive. Based on a review of Campbell's correspondence to the Church, to Beckwith's Washington attorney and to his co-executor at CitiBank, Campbell felt there should not be any difficulty in having the parties sign off on the tangible personal possessions. He was wrong. Obtaining releases from the various interested parties was not going to be easy. He fully realized this on August 9, 1977 when he received a letter from Attorney Young. The tone of Miss Young's letter disclosed that she was not pleased with the way things were being handled. She wrote:

> *I dislike requesting further documents from you but in view of Mr. Beckwith's dual interest in his Sister's Will of legatee and sole heir, Mr. Hill's involvement in the estate as caretaker, Court-appointed appraiser and activist in "Friends of Hildene" and the Court action brought by the Church I think I should now have copies of the two appraisals listed under the heading "Household Furniture" on the summary sheet of the Inventory and would appreciate very much receiving them.*

Attorney Young must not have been aware of the fact that in a small town it was not unusual to experience conflict of interest issues. They are inescapable.

The events being played out among the estate's attorneys began to filter back to Schmid. Representatives of the various legatees were coming to Hildene to identify, pack and ship the specific possessions their employer's were to receive.

Schmid decided that it was now time to summon his executive committee. He had to have a resolution of the issues that had not been

72

resolved since April. And, he had another important issue to add.

· ·

Margaret Dougherty, a Manchester resident, had been a close friend of Peggy's in 1977. She was not a lawyer but she was the State of Vermont's Probate Judge for the Northshire of Bennington County.

The action she took on June 13, 1977 had to have been the most profound of her career as a probate judge. She signed the 'Order' of Decree of Partial Distribution, the second one to be signed on the administering of the estate of Mary Lincoln Beckwith. Only, this time, Judge Dougherty ordered that the title and ownership of Hildene be vested in the Church. There would be no question now that it was the Church who the Friends of Hildene would have to deal with if they wanted to gain possession of the property.

The Decree also transferred $778,882.56 in publicly traded securities as well as those possessions that did not go to Robert Lincoln Beckwith. The Decree made mention of the fact that two items could not be located: The bronze hands of Abraham Lincoln cast from life, and a bridal lace bequeathed to Doris Beckwith.

The court order restated Peggy's wishes for the property. Robert Schmid and Arthur O'Dea were in court to witness the proceedings. They were glum and disappointed, but raised no objections. The size of the endowment the Church was receiving from the estate was a shock to them. They agreed to meet as a group soon. They needed to get on with their mission now that the Church was in possession of a substantial portion of the estate assets. The Church, as far as Schmid and O'Dea were concerned, was now on the offensive. Proof of this momentum was unfolding in a courtroom at the other end of Bennington county. Docket No. S127-77Bc (The Christian Science

Board of Directors v. M. Jerome Diamond et al, Vermont's Attorney General) was plodding its way through the legal system.

On July 13, about a month after the partial distribution, Bob Schmid spoke to Carl Rechner. It was almost five months since the last communication between the Friends of Hildene and the Church. Rechner told Schmid that there would be no further decrease in the price of the property. The price stood unchanged from that which was conveyed to O'Dea in February. However, a request from Rechner to Schmid was made. He wanted to know, in quite specific terms, how the Friends of Hildene would actually use Hildene in the event that they could obtain ownership. Schmid realized the significance of this request. He immediately went to work on drafting a letter to the Church to be presented for approval at the emergency meeting of his trustees.

. . . .

If the Friends of Hildene were experiencing headaches in August of 1977, they were not all being caused by external forces. The pressure to do something was building critically. And at the August 10, 1977 Board of Trustee's meeting, the lid blew off. In his notes, Robert Schmid had referenced the meeting as a "donnybrook". Not all of the nine trustees were there that night. Oscar Johnson, Arthur O'Dea, and William Whitman were absent.

Schmid opened the meeting by having Susan Hill read the minutes of the April 12, 1977 meeting. He then added that

> *The report that Mr. Thum had undertaken to prepare,*
> *relative to disposition of portions of the estate once it had*
> *been acquired, had been prepared and distributed in draft*

74

form to Messrs. Johnson, Schmid, Thum and Friends of Hildene counsel Arthur J. O'Dea, Esq. and it had been decided that the matter would not be pursued at this time.

The basis for dropping this controversial report at this time had been discussed in off-site meetings with individual trustees. It is not known why Schmid's other trustees were never given copies of the report. This omission must have added to the evening's tensions.

Thum added to the gloom by noting that he had only $1,109.91 in the Friends of Hildene checking account. This report was followed by a report from Schmid that final negotiations had been completed with the anonymous donor's attorney. The fact that this was done without Board approval did not sit well with Thum and Carl Saladino. They expressed their objections with regard to matters being dealt with outside of the Board's purview.

Thum's suggestion that the Board of Trustees be increased to include twenty-five trustees was tabled after Romi Perkins suggested that Arthur O'Dea's advice be sought.

Schmid then proposed the names of two new trustees. The follow up discussion went off the record. There would be no problems with one nominee, Gerald Keneally. He would replace William Whitman and/or Carl Saladino. The latter was going back to college. However, Schmid was disappointed when his recommendation of the other nominee, who will remain anonymous, was turned down. He had already assured the nominee of being elected. Schmid was upset. The meeting ended after nearly two hours. It was scheduled to reconvene the following week, in the presence of O'Dea and Oscar Johnson.

Between the two meetings, Schmid went home and spent a good

deal of time reflecting on what had taken place with his Board. He also gave serious thought to the current status of negotiations.

He recalled how deeply hurt he was at the turn of events subsequent to the August 10th meeting. He said, "indeed it was our darkest hour." He discussed with his wife, Mary, the possibility of resigning as Chairman. The cause was not worth the aggravation, the grief and the constant disappointments.

On the other hand, he felt as though he should put these setbacks behind him. He owed it to his wife and others to keep up the struggle to save Hildene. He and others had worked too hard, too long to stop now. He was determined to get through the next meeting, on August 17th, knowing full well that Bob Thum would push hard to get his board restructuring through Trustee approval.

Bob Thum lobbied hard. He circulated a memo to the trustees prior to the meeting outlining his reasons for wanting to restructure the board. He won a partial victory. The Board would stay at nine, but the by-laws would be changed to allow for rotation. O'Dea and Gerald Keneally were nominated for one-year terms to be voted upon at the August 31st annual meeting.

As acrimonious as the two meetings might have been to Schmid and the others present, Schmid held his board intact. The 'family' had aired their frustrations. He then reported one more item to them. He informed them that Carl Rechner had called him to obtain a firm purchase offer from the Friends of Hildene. Schmid and O'Dea were already at work on it. Schmid got the Board to approve their draft of a proposal.

. . . .

76

Within days of his last meeting with the board, Robert Schmid completed a three-page letter to Carl Rechner of the Church. Little did he know when he set pen to paper on August 17, 1977 that his letter would later become "Exhibit C" to a contract between the Church and the Friends of Hildene. On that day he was only concerned with responding promptly to Rechner's August 15th phone call, he had to send the Church a final proposal.

Schmid's letter was clear and succinct. It spelled out the Friends of Hildene's tax exempt status as well as the uses to which the Friends of Hildene planned to put the property to. Schmid noted two main uses:

1) land to the east of River Road would be preserved as prime agricultural land as well as protected wetlands, particularly those lands contiguous to the Battenkill;

2) everything west of River Road and up on the hill would be set aside for Lincoln memorial activities.

It was in the context of his letter to Rechner that Schmid incorporated certain of the suggestions contained in the earlier Bob Thum report to the trustees.

Schmid noted that some of the following activities could be accommodated but that additional feasibility studies needed to be made:

a) an alternative school either within or without public school system;

b) community center for discussion groups, concerts, lectures, film programs and civil celebrations;

c) *research seminars on Lincoln history;*

d) *exhibits of Lincolniana from other collections;*

e) *cooperative programs with area colleges.*

Schmid went on to inform Rechner that Hildene was close to receiving recognition as an historic site through the efforts that were underway by the National Trust for Historic Preservation. He also told Rechner that they were working to secure Federal and State grants regarding the protection of the frontage on the Battenkill River.

Schmid was well aware of the fact that Rechner wanted a 'concrete' offer of purchase. It was all well and good to describe what the Friends of Hildene would do to the property, and how they would do it. But, Rechner really wanted specifics about a deal! Schmid gave him three:

> *Alternative No. I:* *FOH would pay to the Church $100,000 for the entire estate—the 412 acres and the buildings and contents—with our covenant guaranteeing that we would not sell off any part of it, but would devote all of it to public service programs. This is the alternative that we prefer, the one that will enable us to make maximum use of the property to the benefit of the public.*

> *Alternative No. II:* *FOH would pay $200,000 to the Church for the entire estate, but would not be restricted from sale of portions of the land, if such became necessary for financial or advisable for program reasons. FOH would undertake to limit such sale of property to a tax exempt body that would com-*

mit itself to keeping the land open and undeveloped.

Alternative No. III: *FOH would pay $50,000 to the Church for the 255.2 acres of land and the buildings located on those acres west of River Road, limiting its program and the Lincoln memorial to this sector of the estate. The Church, under this option, would be free to sell the 157 acres of valley land to any purchaser who would commit himself, by deed, to keeping the land open and undeveloped.*

The letter was mailed on August 19th. They waited anxiously for Rechner's reply.

Little did the trustees know at the time that while they had been struggling so much amongst themselves, Robert Lincoln Beckwith had been giving away certain Hildene possessions.

On August 16, 1977, he gave to his friend and agent, James Hickey, his grandfather's desk and chair from the Hildene study. This gift was followed a few days later, August 19, 1977, by a gift to the Chicago Public Library. He gave the Library two paintings, one of Robert Todd Lincoln and one of James Harlan.

Hickey was no doubt influential in advising Beckwith as to what should be given away and to whom. It was, in fact, one of the reasons he was retained by Beckwith. To Hickey, it was important for both historical as well as political reasons that the gifts be made to organizations located in his home state of Illinois. A "Sevres" white bisque porcelain bust of Abraham Lincoln was gifted to the Illinois State Historical Library in Springfield. Robert Todd Lincoln had received the bust from the French Republic sixty-seven years earlier.

79

The Chicago Historical Society became the beneficiary of the Hildene clothing collections. To them, on August 19, 1977, Beckwith deeded all of the clothing left at Hildene. The items had once been worn by his grandmother, his aunt Mary and his mother Jessie. The list included:

1.   Two piece lime green satin ball gown
2.   Taffeta (silk) witih padded embroidered floral design dress
3.   Bodice of pink brocade embroidered with pearls, etc.
4.   Ball gown black satin with beading work (unfinished)
5.   Dress of dubonnet satin with braid trim
6.   Dress (large size) black net with sequins
7.   Dress black velvet with jet beading
8.   Dress black net with white beading/velvet blue sash
9.   Dress black net with bugle beads and pearl motif
10. Dress black chiffon with heavily beaded design with red rose
11. Two pieces black net beaded dress
12. White linen parasol
13. Purple silk parasol
14. Light blue parasol with black embroidery, jet beaded handle
15. Shawl of black silk with long fringe
16. Stole of white silk
17. Corset
18. Light blue lounge slippers
19. Black slippers with beading design

20. Headdress

21. Three pieces lace work

22. Two bands pearl network

23. Rhinestone netting panel/blue sequins

24. Two rhinestone netting panels

25. Hat of black straw with roses

26. Silk bonnet (shirred) with ties

27. Hat of white felt/silk trim

28. Two hats ecru colored with black velvet trim

29. Hat of green taffeta (ruffled)

30. Hat of black velvet with jet beading

31. Hat beige felt and velvet with satin ribbon

32. Straw bonnet with dark blue color

33. Hat of red velvet

34. Throat piece of jet beading

35. Stole of black net with silver bugle bead trim

36. Stole of black net with silver thread work

37. Stole of black net with sequin trim

38. Box of jet beading

39. Box hat trimmings (birds)

40. Box of trimmings

41. Piece of velvet with jet-work trim

42. Piece of black satin with beading work

43. Hat pins

This last gift made to the Chicago Historical Society would have important significance in later years. Judith Livingston and Judy Taylor, two long-serving trustees of Hildene, created a Vintage

Clothing Show at Hildene in 1990. The show, which had become a major event, would have been greatly enhanced if it had been able to display the finery of the Lincoln women.

· ·

The August 31, 1977 annual meeting went well for Bob Schmid. He was feeling somewhat euphoric. He told the group about the letter and they gave him his new trustees. O'Dea was elected to the Board of Trustees as well as Gerald Keneally. Keneally was a North Bennington resident and the President of the former Catamount Bank. Along with them a ninth member was added to replace John West. It was Jean Bischoff of Manchester. She was the manager of Harrington's store, located at the corner of Route 11/30 and Route 7a.

· ·

It would be three weeks before Schmid heard back from the Church. On September 13th, he received a call from Rechner. The Church consultant liked the letter of August 19th. He told Schmid to make a formal proposal and send it to him. Schmid sent a memo of the telephone call to his trustees on September 14th. It stated:

1)   Church wanted to sell property in one piece

2)   guarantee to use as a memorial

3)   no sale of property

4)   Church feels that court (decision) will be in their favor, can sell to anyone and [furthermore] we [FOH] do not have claim on $750,000

5) Church is to get credit from Friends of Hildene that Christian Science Church reduced price, in any press release

6) Rechner felt that if we offer $250,000 it would probably be accepted although he is not authorized to make offer

7) the amount would be paid as follows:

   a) $100,000 down
   b) $25,000 each year for six years
   c) no interest
   d) first mortgage on property.

For the first time since Schmid and O'Dea's previous meeting with Rechner in September of 1976, the Friends of Hildene increased the amount of their purchase offer. It went from $165,000 to $250,000. They took the Church up on their offer to take back a long-term mortgage. In this case, it would be for $150,000. The mortgage, together with the $100,000 from their donor, would not exhaust all of their capital but certainly their ability to borrow money. Schmid was well aware of this but he had to be responsive to Rechner's request. Schmid believed that it would be Friends of Hildene's last chance to make a deal happen.

The letter was mailed out on September 28th to Rechner. Schmid also sent a copy to the Friends of Hildene's anonymous donor.

After interacting for six months, after filing a lawsuit and after having received more than one million dollars in cash, securities, real estate, and other Hildene possessions, why did the Church now want to negotiate with the Friends of Hildene?

Schmid had been asked this question by several of his trustees. He responded in writing to all of them by saying:

> *Church has talked with potential other buyer —-*
> *The Church wants to do what is right —-*

Bob Schmid told his Board of Rechner's quote that:

> *"the Bible says that —- 'the love of money is the root of all evil' and the Church does not want to seem greedy"*

One buyer Rechner might have been referring to was Leigh Perkins, President of the Orvis Company. On July 25, 1977, Perkins wrote to the head of the Church's real estate department, Elaine Doherty. Perkins made a proposal to purchase 157 acres along the easterly side of River Road. The real purpose behind the letter was to see if the Church would be willing to split the property. If so, the Friends of Hildene might be able to put on the table a sum of money to acquire the main house, farmhouse and balance of the land.

Schmid had made a similar offer as alternative number three on his August 17th letter. Schmid was unaware of the response Perkins received back from the Church on August 25, 1977.

Rechner answered Perkins' letter by saying:

> *The Church is still looking for one buyer.*

84

Another possibility that was being advanced by Bob Schmid was that the Church was becoming concerned about possibly losing their lawsuit. If so, Robert Beckwith would end up with Hildene. In that scenario, the estate would be taxed. The tax would amount to hundreds of thousands of dollars and its source of payment would be the funds the Church had already received in the June, 1977 distribution. The Church's fears were not totally unfounded.

The Church wanted to get on with the resolution of two items that were haunting them: (1) dealing with the disposition of Hildene and (2) dealing with Robert Beckwith on the issue of personal items and possessions. They would just as soon have the Friends of Hildene deal with him.

. . . .

The period in which the Friends of Hildene's latest offer was being evaluated by the Church was a very nerve-racking time for them. They were not at all sure that the Church was going to be receptive to their offer. They were still not parties to the litigation filed earlier by the Church. It was important that they have some say in the event the case came up for a hearing.

O'Dea, Thum and Schmid believed that the best thing to do was to lay low, "in the bull rushes" as Bob Thum had said. Wait for the Church's response. If no deal was made then the Friends of Hildene would file a consent decree for declaratory judgment. This legal maneuver would incorporate the wishes of all the parties. It would then be brought before Judge Amidon.

The Hildene trustees had also been warned about the growing concerns over possessions of the personal property. They in no way wanted to alienate Robert Beckwith. It was important that they meet

85

with Oscar Johnson and Ken Hill who were much closer to this area of the negotiations than they were.

Hill and Johnson were very concerned as they saw some of Peggy's most precious items being boxed and crated for shipment to Wilson's Storage in Rutland. Neither of them was quite sure as to what items were to go to Robert Beckwith. In late August, Robert Beckwith did not show up for the preparations for the final shipping. He left it in the hands of Hickey and an unnamed woman representative from the Church.

Johnson and Hill's concerns were understandable. For years, during their relationship with Peggy, they were familiar with the items now in boxes. They also wanted the items to remain so that when Hildene was eventually opened to the public they could still see the items just where Peggy had left them.

It was necessary for them to appreciate, that under Peggy's Will, not only was her brother to get certain possessions, but also all of the family's personal items.

Their emotional circumstances were not lost on James Hickey. Over the two years since Peggy's death, a strain had developed between Hill and Hickey — less so between Johnson and Hickey. Oscar recognized that the Friends of Hildene had to abide by the Will. Whatever belonged to Robert Lincoln Beckwith must be given to him. By maintaining this positive position, his actions would later result in having numerous items returned to Hildene.

Schmid, on the other hand, was told by Campbell to back off from his aggressive stance in his attempt to block R.L. Beckwith and his agent from removing from the estate what was rightfully theirs. This order from Campbell came on the same day, May 17, 1977, that

Campbell had written to Beckwith's attorney and told her that

the Friends wanted everything they could lay their hands on.

Campbell must have received notice from Robert Beckwith and James Hickey who were at Hildene during the month of April.

Schmid did not back off so easily. He followed up with a letter to Campbell on May 20, 1977:

> *Just after telling you on the telephone yesterday that I would hold off on further expressions of concern over the disposition of the furnishings, documents and memorabilia at Hildene, I thought of a specific item that probably deserves special attention: namely, the small painting by Rosa Bonheur.*

Schmid was insistent and wanted to go on record with his feelings concerning the possessions still at Hildene. He went on to say:

> *This is an example of the "contents" of the house that we believe rightfully belong, under the will, to the Christian Science Church and that the Church has told us it will include in the "package" when we finally come to terms over the sale of the property to Friends of Hildene; hence, I feel that Friends of Hildene has a real and legitimate interest in protecting this item of property and the other furnishings, papers and memorabilia. ...*

Campbell had a sense that he and his co-executor, Emil Lemay, were losing control of the Robert Lincoln Beckwith inheritance issue.

While holding the Friends of Hildene at bay, he had to spend time both at Hildene and in Rutland to inspect what was going to Robert Beckwith's home in Virginia. He wanted both the Church and his counter-part in New York City to come to Vermont and do likewise. On October 19, 1977 Campbell finally reached Phil Hunt, legal counsel for the Church. In a letter the following day to Lemay at Citibank he wrote:

> *... It appears that the Church is still dickering with the Friends of Hildene, and he said that if they come to an agreement, the Church proposes to turn the whole matter over to the Friends to settle any controversy with Mr. Robert T.L. Beckwith. ...*

Campbell wanted his job as executor to be over. He did not want to continue dealing with a group of local residents who he believed would not be able to buy Hildene. He also envisioned the potential for litigation that would arise if the Friends of Hildene were in a bargaining position and had to deal with Robert Beckwith, Elizabeth Young and James Hickey. He went on to say in his letter to Lemay:

> *... I do not think we should consent to substituting the Friends of Hildene for the Church insofar as releases are concerned. ...*

Campbell was not going to have a choice. He was going to have to deal with the Friends of Hildene.

Carl Rechner of the Christian Science Church phoned Schmid on October 19th and told the Friends of Hildene chairman that the Church accepted the offer of $200,000 plus a $50,000 mortgage. And, further, that a contract to purchase would arrive in Vermont within two weeks.

· ·

The contract arrived on November 2, 1977. Schmid and the others were euphoric even if more cash was required. They had succeeded. Their dream had come true. Hildene was not going to be sold to others. It was going to belong to the people and be a memorial to Peggy's mother and grandparents.

On November 13th, the contract was mailed to the trustees and to the attorneys for the anonymous donor. The call Bob Schmid received on November 18th from O'Dea was shocking. The donor, he was told, was going to renege. The $200,000 would not be forthcoming.

· ·

It took Bob Schmid and Art O'Dea nearly nine months to solidify the arrangement with the attorneys for the anonymous donor. When they read the letter of November 15, 1977 from Middleton Miller, an attorney with the Washington, D.C. and Chicago law firm of Sidley and Austin, they were devastated.

Miller said:

> ... *In my view the proposed agreement [with the Church] is totally unsatisfactory from the Donor's standpoint.*

Miller went on to state:

> *... I think the Donor would be on firm ground in refusing to make the payment under the circumstances of the proposed agreement. ...*

The long drawn out agreement with the donor made clear that all of the $200,000 was to go to the purchase of Hildene — not for part of the estate and not with mortgage liens as Schmid and O'Dea would learn on that mid-November morning. Hildene's attorney was told that

> *the donor will not be a party to any agreement, will not honor the pledge as long as the contract with the Church has a mortgage lien on the Hildene property. ...*

The concern here, of course, was that if the Friends of Hildene were to fail in their attempt to make Hildene into the place they had planned, the Church could step in and take over the property. If that scenario were to happen, the donor's $200,000 grant would have been wasted.

Also, on November 14, 1977 the donor's Manchester attorney, Sydney Meachem of Evans, O'Neil and Meachem, Ltd., wrote to O'Dea and Middleton Miller. Miller made a constructive suggestion. If the Church was willing to waive the interest on the note [mortgage] for five years, would they consider taking less if it was an all cash deal?

Five days later, on November 23rd, Schmid placed the problem and suggestion before Rechner. The Church's real estate consultant was livid. He thought the Church and the Friends of Hildene had made a deal. He wondered if he could trust these people. Schmid was willing to have him contact Attorney Miller. He did not have to. On December 6th, Attorney Hunt called Schmid and O'Dea and told them that the Church would accept $200,000. O'Dea immediately informed Miller and Meachem. They were pleased. The donor's problem was resolved.

· ·

What surely had helped these discussions and negotiations along was the filing of a motion in Bennington's Superior Court by Arthur O'Dea.

The original Motion to Intervene that had been prepared by O'Dea in response to the Church's motion for declaratory judgment had never been filed. Instead, on November 28th, O'Dea filed a motion for "leave to intervene." It stated:

> *Petition of Intervenor is not being filed at this time and this Motion will not be moved for hearing until such time as said negotiations are concluded.*

The good news followed on the heels of Hildene's being placed on the National Trust for Historic Preservation. Additional Federal and State funds could now flow to the Friends of Hildene for renovation and restoration work.

Schmid needed to call for a full meeting of his trustees. They had to ratify the contract. This had to be accomplished before year's end. He also had to inform them that on December 13th Robert Beckwith submitted his resignation as Honorary Chairman of the Board of Trustees. It would be early in the following year that the

Friends of Hildene and the Church would be hearing from Mr. Beckwith's Vermont attorney. Meanwhile, Bob Thum was authorized by the Board of Trustees to sign the Purchase Agreement on behalf of the Friends of Hildene.

· ·

Sixteen months from the time the Friends of Hildene was formed to save Hildene, a contract was executed. On December 27, 1977, Robert 'Bob' Thum carried out the task for the Friends of Hildene.

For Bob Thum, it was a special moment. He and his wife, Millie, had moved to Dorset in January of 1976 from Cleveland, Ohio. He became involved with Hildene because he was a Civil War buff and knew O'Dea from the work the attorney had done for the Town of Dorset.

The eight-page Purchase and Sale Agreement, together with three attached schedules (Schedule C being Robert Schmid's letter of August 19, 1977), was executed for the Church by DeWitt John, its acting Chairman of the Board of Directors, on December 30, 1977.

Without the benefit of having witnessed what had transpired since July 1976, a reading of the fourth paragraph of the agreement would cause one to conclude that all along there must have been a pleasant and cordial series of negotiations between the Church and the Friends of Hildene:

... WHEREAS, the Church early encouraged the formation of a local group which might qualify to acquire the property under appropriate terms and conditions such that the wishes and directions of the Testatrix might be carried out and the local community might benefit therefrom and Friends is the only

group which has evolved from local initiative; and ....

The contract went on to describe certain restrictions that the Friends of Hildene needed to follow:

1) *The property must not be used as a medical facility or hospital.*

2) *Alcoholic beverages could not be sold on the property. They could be consumed only as an ancillary or accessory activity to any proper function.*

3) *Because of the below-market selling price, no part of the property could be sold for twenty years.*

The contract between the Friends of Hildene and the Church was signed. All that remained to be done was for Art O'Dea to send to the Church the $20,000 deposit. He had until January 10, 1978 to have the funds in the hands of the Church.

The anonymous donor had been satisfied with the contract's new terms. O'Dea called the donor's attorney for the down payment of $20,000. He received that amount on January 9th as a deposit into his law firm's trust account and on January 12th he wrote a check to the Church — the contract was official. All the parties had to do now, they thought, was to wait for the Vermont Superior Court to agree to the sale by the Church to the Friends of Hildene. A closing was then to take place within thirty days.

• •

Once Bob Schmid realized that there was to be a deal with the Church, he began to search for a full time director of Hildene. A breakthrough came in early December of 1977. On December 5, 1977, David Sheldon arrived at Hildene. The mid-westerner had read about Hildene and the negotiations with the Church.

Sheldon, who was at the time the Executive Director of the YMCA facility in Glen Ellyn, Illinois, was so sure of obtaining the position that when he showed up for the interview with Schmid his automobile license plate read F.O.H. [Friends of Hildene]. The fifty-year-old Sheldon possessed a Master's degree in Religious Education from the McCormick Theological Seminary in Chicago as well as a B.A. in Sociology. He would be hired on March 3rd the following year. He was given living quarters in the main house. Schmid wished he had come sooner — on February 3rd, Schmid and his colleagues mailed out 10,000 letters in a national fundraising effort. The list of names was obtained from an anonymous source. According to Schmid, the list was of high quality. Through the use of computer sorting, names were selected as candidates for letters.

While the Friends of Hildene were relishing their euphoria, little did they know that others were at work attempting to undo the recently signed Purchase and Sale Agreement.

On January 20, 1978, approximately a week after the Friends of Hildene sent their deposit for the Agreement to the Church, James Hickey, the curator of the Lincoln Collection of the Illinois State Historical Library, wrote to Peter Holden. A Bennington attorney, Holden had been retained by Elizabeth Young, Robert Lincoln Beckwith's Washington attorney.

The purpose of Hickey's letter was to inform Holden about the disposition of certain personal possessions that he and Mr. Beckwith had removed from Hildene. Also, Hickey wanted Holden to know about one John R. Gehlbach.

> *... Mr. John R. Gehlbach has called Mr. Hunt [attorney for the Christian Science Church] and offered to buy Hildene Estate at more than the price being paid by 'Friends of Hildene' and to purchase the contents at the appraisal price. Mr. Gehlbach is a friend of Mr. Beckwith's and would not object to his having from the house those items he wants. Mr. Gehlbach has or will make this offer in a letter to Mr. Hunt. Mr. Hunt did not disclose or admit to Mr. Gehlbach that they had an agreement to purchase with 'Friends of Hildene'. ...*

Mr. Gehlbach was from Elkhart, llinois. He was an attorney and a trustee of Mr. Hickey's Library. Years later, on July 30, 1993, he and Mr. Hickey were at the Equinox Hotel in Manchester, Vermont. They were there in connection with the Lincoln Family Symposium that was being sponsored by the Friends of Hildene.

During a recess, Gehlbach and Hickey were asked about the January 1978 letter. For both of them, it was an event from 'long ago'. At the time they had felt as though the Peggy Beckwith estate could very well be lost, that the Friends of Hildene might not be able to save it. It had dragged on too long. Hickey stated this in his 1977 letter:

> *... I believe if it had not been for the 'Friends of Hildene' who are really not a party to the settlement of this estate, Mr. Beckwith, the Church, and the executors could have reached agreement long ago. ...*

Hickey's letter never mentioned another purchaser. They offered $250,000 to the Church. They were only interested in the main house and the surrounding land. It would have been their intention to sell off all of the other lands. Their offer was never accepted for obvious reasons. Furthermore, Hickey noted that his and Gehlbach's attempt to purchase Hildene should be made known. They believed it was part of the story to save Hildene. Jim Hickey died in June, 1996.

· ·

For the Friends of Hildene, the joy and enthusiasm that began the year of 1978 were soon to disappear. The significance attached to the signing of the purchase agreement, the receipt of the anonymous donor's first advance, the mailing of thousands of fundraising letters and the hiring of a full time professional director faded on February 3rd, when the Friends of Hildene heard about Peter Holden's letter to Jonathan Bump, the Brattleboro, Vermont attorney for the Church.

Peter Holden, Esq., continues to practice law in Bennington, Vermont. In 1977, he was appointed by Elizabeth Young, Esq. to represent Mr. Beckwith's interests in Vermont. At that time he was a partner with the law firm of Clark, Lillie and Holden. Although he never met Mr. Beckwith, Holden was to play a crucial role in the negotiations with the Friends of Hildene on behalf of his client.

His role took on serious proportions on January 25, 1978 when he received a telephone call from Attorney Campbell. The co-executor had alerted Holden to a meeting Campbell had in his office with Bob Thum on December 26, 1977, the day before Thum had signed the Purchase and Sale Agreement.

At their meeting, Thum had outlined to Campbell certain items that he felt had been taken from Hildene by Beckwith which properly belonged to the Church and would accordingly be coming to the Friends of Hildene when the contract was closed. Campbell reduced the list of items to writing. Campbell went on to tell Holden that Thum said that the Friends of Hildene would be willing to negotiate with Mr. Beckwith. Thum suggested that the items could rotate among the various locations — Virginia, Illinois and Hildene. Holden, only a few days prior, had received a three-page letter from Mr. Hickey, Beckwith's agent. When Holden received Campbell's letter on January 25, 1978, he became quite upset. Elizabeth Young had some time earlier informed Holden that Hickey represented Mr. Beckwith's interest. Hickey, in his January 20, 1978 letter to Holden, stated:

> *... I believe I am correct in saying that Mr. Beckwith does not intend to give, sell or trade any item to the 'Friends of Hildene,' that almost all of the items he is getting, he has or will give to various historical agencies. We would hope that an agreement can be reached so that he will not be bothered by 'Friends of Hildene' or anyone else who may acquire Hildene for any item or items he has removed or has been removed for him, or item which he is now asking for. ...*

Holden was aware of the fact that, only two weeks prior, Elizabeth Young had requested and received an amended contract. She had been upset with Article Eight of the contract between the Church and Friends of Hildene that named her client as Honorary Chairman of the Friends of Hildene. Earlier in December her client had resigned. She wanted his name removed. It was done.

Holden, on February 3, 1978, wrote to the Attorney for the

Church, Jonathan Bump. He noted:

> *... It is my understanding that the Friends of Hildene have already raised questions concerning Mr. Beckwith's removal of items which they claim. ...*

Attorney Holden went on to state:

> *... Given the cloudy status of the personal property situation, we feel that it would be most ill-advised for the proposed sale to be consummated before a clear understanding among all interested parties has been reached concerning the proper ownership of these items. ...*

Robert Beckwith's attorney realized what Campbell had already told the Church and his co-executor months before — which was:

> *... We do not wish to be put in the position of negotiating after the fact with the Friends of Hildene. Ownership of the personal property is a matter which properly should be resolved between the Church, the estate, and Mr. Beckwith. ...*

Holden said he would put together a list of all those items that his client was entitled to under Article Second and Seventh of the Will. Further, he wanted all parties to agree to such a list (he obviously meant the Church and the Friends of Hildene). In the event that the parties could not agree, Holden put forth the following:

> *... Absent such an agreement, however, we will have no alternative but to seek the court's guidance as to the 'personal effects' clause and we will not foreclose the possibility of raising an objection to the proposed sale itself on the ground that it is not consonant with the intention of the testatrix. ...*

PART V: THE SETTLEMENT

Within a month, on March 1, 1978, having not heard from Hunt, Holden would write to him again. This time he was willing, on behalf of his client, to concede certain personal items as long as those items on the Master List were attended to by the Church and the Friends of Hildene. Hunt, in turn, forwarded the Beckwith Master List to Schmid and O'Dea. Despite Campbell's protestations, he wanted nothing to do with the personal property issue — he wanted the Friends of Hildene to resolve the problem.

In a two-page letter from O'Dea to Holden dated March 14, 1978, O'Dea noted that the Friends of Hildene were interested in a prompt resolution of the matter. He went on to make the following points:

1) [The Friends of Hildene] Waive any claim regarding those items Beckwith wanted to purchase from the Church.
2) The Friends of Hildene would be in great need of Hildene's building plans, maps and photos.
3) Leave at Hildene the sundial and telescope. (The latter had already been given to Burr & Burton Seminary in Manchester by Peggy.)

O'Dea's letter was conciliatory in nature. He wanted the issue to be brought to an end without litigation. He continued:

... a number of items on the Master List would be of benefit to the Friends of Hildene in carrying out their mission, but we are willing to waive them ...

O'Dea, for whatever reason, asked in his letter for a discretionary donation from Holden's client. Nothing was received — at that time.

· ·

O'Dea's letter paid dividends. The parties were about to settle. The antagonistic feelings that had passed between Beckwith, Hickey, the Church and the Friends of Hildene were about to subside. On April 4, 1977, O'Dea received a draft amendment to the December 30, 1977 purchase agreement between Friends of Hildene and the Church. The amendment read as follows:

WHEREAS certain aspects of the Agreement of Purchase and Sale dated December 30, 1977 are unclear, and the parties wish to avoid any possible confusion by elaborating on the original Agreement;

THEREFORE, said Agreement of Purchase and Sale is Amended as follows:

1. Paragraph 8 of said Agreement is Amended to read as follows:

Under Paragraphs Second and Seventh of the Will, testatrix made provision for Robert Lincoln Beckwith, her brother. It is understood that the Church will convey only such interest as it may have in the personal property described in Schedule B. Friends agree to hold the Church harmless from any liability, costs and legal fees incurred by the Church with respect to any claims made against such property. It is agreed that the Church does not hereby convey any interest in any of the personal property which is listed on the

"Beckwith Master List", *attached hereto as Exhibit D, as being the property of Robert Beckwith.*

By April 24th all parties had signed off. O'Dea told Sydney Meachem, the donor's attorney, of the good news. It was now time to have the Court sign off. A Stipulation Agreement had to be drafted and filed with the Court.

The Stipulation, or motion, had to have the signatures of the Friends of Hildene, the Church, Robert Lincoln Beckwith, and also the Vermont Attorney General. In essence, by signing such an agreement the parties were informing the Court that they had among themselves resolved their differences and, as such, would the Court agree to what they had arrived at in such settlement.

. . . .

The moment of truth was getting closer for the Friends of Hildene. In two months they would be the owners of Hildene. Then what? They needed more help. It had been proposed that an Advisory Board be formed. Bob Schmid wrote in the Hildene newsletter that:

> ... *We are fortunate to be able to strengthen our organization at this time by the accession of these good citizens. In the very near future we will be facing some key decisions in the administration of the Robert Todd Lincoln estate, and we will depend heavily on the experience and good judgment of our Advisory Board. ...*

In June the Trustees gave him the following Advisory Board members, some of whom would later play key roles when the Friends of Hildene moved into their next phase:

Stig Albertsson	Judy Taylor
Mary Bort	John Trethaway
Reverend Jerome Hevey, Jr.	Henry van Loon
Tony Perry	Dr. Ilsley S. Zecher

· ·

Not everyone was optimistic that the Friends of Hildene would be able to close on the property, even at this late date - June 1978. This feeling was especially expressed by Attorney Campbell.

Campbell, on June 13, 1978, wrote to Elizabeth Young, Robert Lincoln Beckwith's attorney, and told her that he would not accept a receipt of personal property from the Friends of Hildene but insisted it come from the Church and that he did not blame Mr. Beckwith for "grumbling." He went on to say that:

> *... There seems to be some doubt that Friends of Hildene can come up with the purchase price for the property. As near as I can determine, there seems to be very little local support for the organization. ...*

He also provided future historians with a trail to be followed in connection with any biography on Peggy. He told Miss Young:

> *... I have been unable to find any reference in Miss Beckwith's files here in the office to Mr. [Robert] Beckwith's father's estate. Most of Miss Beckwith's personal papers were taken to New York by Citibank. I will write to the Bank to see if they can come up with anything. ...*

· ·

104

Almost one year to the date that the Church had filed their law suit, June 6, 1978, Attorney Bump on behalf of the Church asked Vermont's Assistant Attorney General, Michael Gadue, to sign the Stipulation. All of the parties had already done so.

On June 20, 1978, before Judge Amidon, the struggle by a small group of Manchester residents was brought to a successful conclusion. The Judge executed the motion for summary judgment. All that remained to be done was for O'Dea to check the title of the property. He did this over a two week period between June 22, 1978 and July 7, 1978. There were no problems. A closing date was established.

· ·

"... We are grateful that this agreement has been worked out so that Miss Beckwith's friends and neighbors could carry out her wishes for Hildene. ..."

Manchester Journal August 3, 1978

So said Robert Wade at the closing of the Purchase and Sale Agreement between the Friends of Hildene and the Church.

Wade was the Church's Vermont representative. He represented Carl Rechner that day. He read from a statement that was prepared by Rechner.

The closing took place in the dining room at Hildene on July 27, 1978. Quite fittingly, it was at the dining room table — with a portrait of Robert Todd Lincoln looking down at the proceedings, most likely wondering what all the fuss was about.

Wade went on to say:

... The approval granted at Bennington June 20 [1978] by the

Superior Court with the full cooperation of the Attorney General of Vermont and of Miss Beckwith's surviving brother, Robert Lincoln Beckwith, brings the disposition of his unique property to a most gratifying conclusion. ...

Gathered around the large cherry dining room table along with O'Dea and listening to Wade were:

Jonathan Bump, Esq.	Jean Bischoff
Robert Schmid	Stig Albertsson
Oscar Johnson	Rev. Jerome Hevey, Jr.
Ken Hill	John Trethaway
Romi Perkins	Judy Taylor
Gerald Keneally	Mary Bort
Robert Thum	Dr. Ilsley Zecher

They, together with the reporters, witnessed the lawyers carrying out the closing rituals. Deeds and maps were reviewed. Lists of furniture, equipment and furnishings were checked for completeness. Allocation of the electric bill, oil, and real estate taxes led to serious discussions and negotiations.

Wade wasn't finished reading Rechner's remarks.

It took many months to reach this agreement. There was a natural desire on the part of the Directors [of the Church] to accommodate the aspirations of the local community for constructive public use of this notable estate. And, of course, the directors sought to observe the spirit as well as the letter of the bequest. ...

It was critically important for the Church to have the opportunity to make such a statement. They were not unaware of the publicity and impact it would have on future donors to the Church.

The Church also insisted that the transaction be treated in two parts — a purchase for $200,000 by the Friends of Hildene and a gift from the Christian Science Church to the Friends of Hildene for $425,000. The Friends of Hildene had no difficulty in accepting this treatment. Doug Shaw had appraised the property in 1976 at that amount. Much had to be done — August 4th was set as Dedication Day.

· ·

The Dedication ceremony on August 4, 1978 and the ribbon cutting ceremony that was held on September 18th headed up by Governor Snelling of Vermont, marked the beginning of the next phase for the Friends of Hildene. Their work continues to this day. Hildene recently opened to visitors for its 25th tour season. Well over a million and a half visitors have toured the house and grounds or have attended the numerous special events that are an annual ritual on the 412-acre estate. Among the special events are concerts, high school proms, polo matches, antique shows and craft fairs. Also held at the Hildene meadowlands is an annual antique car show. Another event is the annual farm, food and craft fair where animals of all sizes and shapes are exhibited. Probably the most cherished events are the numerous weddings held in the gardens at the Main House. Hildene has truly been opened to the public.

Hildene's permanent staff of nine is headed up by Gerrit Kouwenhoven who succeeded Dave Sheldon as Executive Director in 1985. Backing up the staff is a corps of volunteers, numbering three hundred fifty. The number of Trustees chosen each year was increased to nineteen. The Advisory Board was increased to seventeen.

The restoration of Hildene's twenty-five plus buildings and grounds is an on-going venture. As of 2001, after twenty-three years, the combined blessings of the generosity of over 2,500 members, the special gifts (no Federal or State monies) and the thousands of hours of volunteer time have restored the property to an almost miraculous appearance.

The Friends of Hildene never received any of Peggy's cash or securities that went to the Church. One can only wonder what would have transpired if it had. Would Hildene in 2001 still have been as successful as it is today? —- Probably not. The common thread that is so evident in the staff, volunteers, advisors and trustees is their dedication to the place Peggy wanted as a memorial to her mother and grandparents. All one has to do to see and live this experience is to take a tour of the main house or attend a Hildene-sponsored function.

When Attorney Campbell and his co-executor filed the estate's final accounting on February 8, 1978, they reported that the total value of Mary Lincoln Beckwith's estate was $1,786,897.16. Of that amount, $1,535,508.07 went to the Church and $13,685 went to Mary E. Colonna Schmid, Alice Colonna and Robert Todd Lincoln Beckwith. The latter receiving $8,685 worth of property in lieu of cash.

With hindsight, the Church was correct in their keeping the endowment. It was rightfully theirs. The Friends of Hildene have done well when they have had to struggle. And struggle they did. The Church also deserves credit for their insistence on keeping the property intact — despite the best intentions from so many individuals and groups, including the Friends of Hildene, to divide it up into smaller parcels in order to accommodate the purchase.

Had Peggy executed her revised Will, dated February 2, 1974, the distribution and the legatees would have been different. But she didn't sign it. Instead, a few courageous souls took up the challenge to save Hildene. How much richer they have become for their work! How rich we all are today for the work the Friends of Hildene undertook on that summer night in July of 1976! We are all a great deal richer than the simple number shown on the estate's final accounting statement. The fact is, Hildene's value today cannot be quantified.

At dedication, Oscar V. Johnson Jr., Peter Brooks and David Sheldon
at Hildene's flag pole.

Arthur O'Dea, Hildene's Attorney passing check to the church representative, Robert Wade. L to R – O'Dea, Oscar Johnson, Ken Hill, Robert Schmid, Robert Thum, Wade.

Robert Schmid signing documents at closing and his Board of Trustees Witnessing

Governor Richard Snelling cutting the ribbon to formally open
Hildene in 1978.

EPILOGUE

The Original Board of Trustees

At a University of Vermont President's installation ceremony, Former Vermont Governor Salmon said:

"We have not inherited this institution from our predecessors. Instead, we have borrowed it from our children."

The meaning of the words spoken by Governor Salmon can well be applied to the intentions and deeds of Hildene's original Board of Trustees.

ROBERT TODD LINCOLN BECKWITH gave as his reason for relinquishing the title Honorary Chairman of the Board of Trustees, his other commitments and that there would be too much public exposure. In 1981 he married his long time friend Margaret Fristoe. Over the years he sent back to Hildene many precious items of historical nature. He died on December 24, 1985 at his farm in Woodstock, Virginia ... the last of Abraham Lincoln's descendants.

ROBERT SCHMID stepped down as Chairman in December of 1979. He and his wife, Mary, moved to Hanover, New Hampshire, just around the corner from Dartmouth College. Now eighty-five, Bob enjoys being retired and still has fond memories of his days and nights in carrying out his responsibilities as Hildene's first president and Chairman of the Board. He was named a Trustee Emeritus in 1980, and in 1996 he and Mary moved to Sarasota, Florida.

In 1993 ARTHUR J. O'DEA, ESQ. retired after ten years of service as a Vermont State Judge. He continues to practice law and is the founder of Vermont Dispute Resolution Service, a firm dedicated to the settlement of disputes through mediation. He and his wife, Bobbie, operate the Whimsy Farm Bed & Breakfast in Arlington, Vermont. When he was appointed a Judge, he was made a Trustee Emeritus. His younger brother, Joseph O'Dea, a Manchester attorney, served as chairman of the Board of Trustees between 1998-2000. And also acts as Hildene's attorney.

OSCAR V. JOHNSON, JR. succeeded Bob Schmid as Chairman. He held that position until 1992, when he elected to step down and was succeeded by Judith Livingston. During his tenure as Chairman, Hildene experienced phenomenal growth in attendance, volunteers, programs, and in stature. He was awarded an honorary Doctorate degree from Lincoln College in Lincoln, Illinois on May 11, 1985. In 1993 the Hildene Visitors' Center (formerly the pony barn) was renamed the 'Oscar V. Johnson, Jr. Visitor's Center.'

At ninety years, Oscar can be seen, during the growing season, atop his tractor mower, cutting the putting green in front of his late and dear friend Peggy's home. He was made Chairman Emeritus in 1992. He and his wife Cecelia (who for many years volunteered at the Hildene gift shop) still live on their farm on River Road just below Robert Todd Lincoln's Hildene.

ROBERT THUM died on March 10, 1992. He served Hildene

right up to the day he died. Bob continued as Treasurer for many years after the Friends of Hildene acquired the property. His intelligent and shrewd stewardship, of the ever so scarce funds, was what was needed during that period. He is, however, best remembered by those who heard his skill in playing Hildene's Aeolian organ, which, in 1992, was named the Robert Thum Memorial Organ and an endowment fund established. To have followed Bob on one of his many tours of the Main House was a memorable experience and to have heard him describe the founding years of the Friends of Hildene was worth the price of the tour pass.

His presence is still felt at Hildene, especially when his widow, Millie Thum, and their son Frank visit the place Bob had loved so dearly. A concert on the lawn near the Main House is held each summer in his honor.

SUSAN HILL continued to serve as a trustee well into the 1980s. Her services, although lost to Hildene, are continuously given to other Manchester non-profit organizations. In the early 1990s she opened up her own accounting firm where she practices her skill as a certified public accountant.

KEN HILL died on February 14, 1999. Almost fifty-three years from when Peggy first hired him, he was active at Hildene. Ken was employed during the tour season as "House Captain and Docent." Almost all of Hildene's docents were in some fashion trained and educated in their role by Ken.

For the Hills, whose roots in the area go back to the late 1700s, Hildene is truly a family affair. Ken's widow, Lois, could be seen at

Hildene during the tour season. Her tours were laced with anecdotes of her family's experiences and personal relationships with Peggy. She passed away in August 2001.

ROMI PERKINS to this day cannot get Hildene out of her sights, literally. She and her husband, Leigh, restored the Walter Hard house on River Road and have a clear view of Hildene's cliffs and main house from their front porch. Romi, one of Hildene's longest tenured Board members was given Trustee Emeritus status in April, 2000.

CARL SALADINO left the Board in August of 1977 to pursue his education at the University of Vermont. Later, his family moved from Manchester.

JOHN WEST left the Board of Trustees in August of 1977. It had been a tremendously busy year for him. He was co-chair of Manchester's Bi-Centennial Commission. He also was heavily involved in the area's Little League program and was a founder of Manchester's Green-up and Blue-up Day.

His commitment to the Friends of Hildene and the saving of the estate pre-dated the Friends of Hildene's first meeting. During his career as Manchester Village Road Commissioner he often helped his friend Peggy, especially in keeping her mile long drive opened. John died on January 25, 1979.

WILLIAM WHITMAN, who was in his late twenties when he joined the Friends of Hildene brought the same tenacity and dedication to their struggle as he did a decade before as a Navy Corpsman serving with the U.S. Marines in Viet-Nam. His family's roots to Hildene went back to his grandfather and grandmother — they both worked for Robert Todd Lincoln as coachman and house servant respectively. Their marriage in the early days of Hildene must have been the first of what would later become a tradition. Bill still has some of the pieces of a silver set given to his grandparents as a wedding gift by their employer, Robert Todd Lincoln.

Bill left the Board in August of 1977. He needed the time to complete his full time degree in management and economics at Castleton College. He would later marry Carol (Hosley). They have two sons. He and his family live in Orange Park, Florida where Bill is employed by the Navy Department.

CREDITS FOR PHOTOGRAPHY

Many of the photographs used in this book were provided with permission by :

The Bennington Banner

Beula Cornelius Nunn

Friends of Hildene, Inc.

My thanks to all and especially to Colonel Albert C. Jerman, USAF (RET) for the photographs used on the front and back covers.

• Throughout the book, all references to the Church means
The First Church of Christ, Scientist.